Soldier By Chance

Memories of Vietnam

Thomas White

Manzanita Writers Press
Angels Camp, California

Soldier By Chance: Memories of Vietnam
By Thomas White

Copyright ©2020 Thomas White

ISBN: 978-0-9986910-5-3

Library of Congress: 2020933243

All rights reserved. No part of this book, neither prose nor photographs, may be reproduced, distributed, or transmitted in any form or by any means, including photocopying, recording, or other electronic or mechanical methods, without the prior written permission of the publisher, except in the case of brief quotations embodied in critical reviews and certain other noncommercial uses permitted by copyright law. For permission requests, write to the publisher, addressed "Attention: Permissions Coordinator," at the address below.

This book is published by:

Manzanita Writers Press
PO Box 215
San Andreas, CA 95249

manzanitawp@gmail.com

Manzapress.com

Book Design and Photo Restoration - David Vassar

Cover Art - David Vassar with Joyce Dedini

*To my Dad, his brothers,
and all who served.*

Author, Thomas White, in Dong Ha, Vietnam - 1967

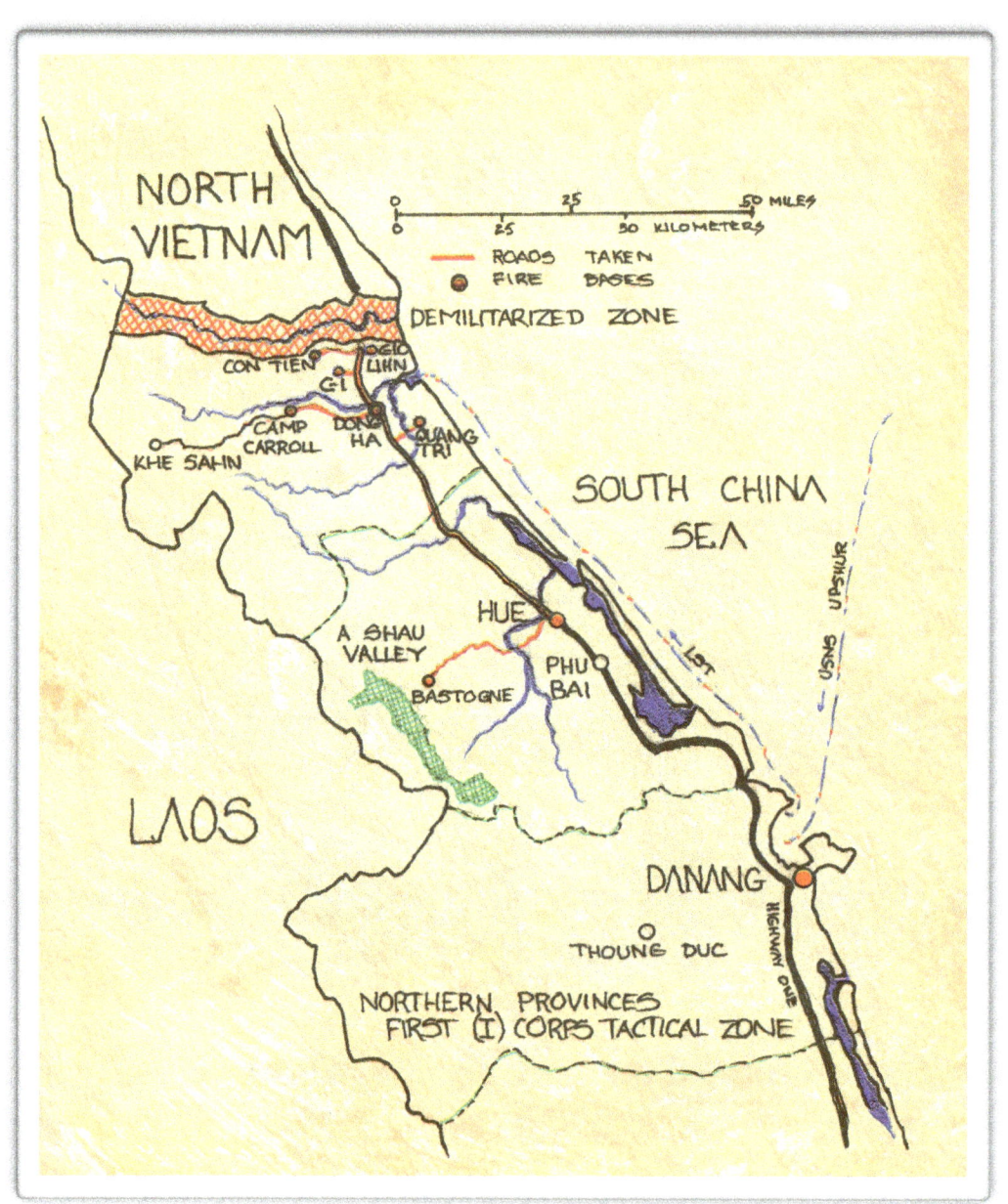

Map of I-Corps, South Vietnam by Thomas White

ACKNOWLEDGMENTS

First and foremost, I must thank my partner Priscilla White for tolerating my departure from the present to reenter the past. I am also grateful to David Vassar for his instrumental help in book design and photo restoration. Monika Rose, Sally Kaplan, and Joyce Dedini of Manzanita Writers Press also contributed to the writing, editing, and design of this book. Funding for editorial and publishing costs was graciously provided by my sister Cynthia Holbach and a grant from the Calaveras County Arts Council. A special thanks to Kathy Mazzaferro for her support. Gratitude to Gateway Press for their assistance. Some valuable information from Michael McDaniel, USMC, deserves thanks as well.

PHOTO NOTES

Unless otherwise credited, all photographs are by Thomas White and soldiers of Charlie Battery, 8th Battalion, 4th Artillery, US Army.

The sourced images include 35mm Ektachrome and Kodachrome color slides, 35mm black & white negatives, and scans from color and black & white prints. Given that the photographs are more than fifty years old, care has been taken to eliminate dirt and scratches and to rebalance color to achieve an accurate restoration of the original images, while at the same time preserving their inherent vintage. Tom's photos were shot with a Canon 35mm SLR, that he lost in Da Nang.

The two photographs from Bastogne, Pages 143 & 147 are provided with kind permission from the collection of Ryan P. Niebuhr, 2nd Infantry Brigade, Airborne Division, US Army.

.175-millimeter, self propelled gun - Dong Ha, Vietnam

INTRODUCTION

I arrived in Vietnam with the 8th Battalion, 4th Artillery, in July of 1967. We left Da Nang and began our journey to the Demilitarized Zone (DMZ) dividing South and North Vietnam. The Vietnamese on the opposite sides of this political boundary had more in common than those separated by the Mason Dixon Line during our own Civil War. Politics created the DMZ and the ensuing conflict. The policies of the Soviet Union and China influenced North Vietnam, while the United States supported South Vietnam in its efforts to avert a Communist takeover. This created the perfect atmosphere for war.

My Army .175mm gun battery spent most of its time close to the DMZ in Marine fire bases. The 175 was not in the Marine's arsenal. Our mission was considerably different from the infantry. We did not leave the compounds on patrol or chopper into hostile territory to capture a hill. For us, direct contact with the enemy was infrequent. From our firebases, we sent 156-pound projectiles their way. The exhilaration of war that we experienced was in response to our adversaries' primary purpose of hurling their big projectiles back at us.

The events that take place on the following pages are fairly accurate, given the passage of time. A few of the names have been changed to protect the guilty, or they have simply been forgotten. This is an account of Charlie Battery's time in Vietnam from July 1967 to August 1968. I have a particular Vietnam story to tell, and I hope this book accomplishes that mission.

Thomas White
December 2020

CONTENTS

FORT SILL - OKLAHOMA	13
SAN FRANCISCO	23
U.S. NAVAL SHIP *UPSHUR*	27
OKINAWA	32
D - DAY	34
DONG HA	38
FIRING SEQUENCE FOR .175-MM GUN	41
CHINA BEACH	55
QUANG TRI	57
CAM LO - CAMP CARROLL	65
A GOOD DEED GONE BAD	68
HOW DID I GET HERE?	71
CHARLIE - 1	74
BATTERY MOVES IN	79
CON TIEN	84
INCOMING - THE SIEGE	91
SANDBAG RUN	97
HUANG ON	102
BAD DAY AT C-1	107
NAVY DROPS IN	109

SIEGE ENDS	110
DENTIST	116
LAUNDRY DETAIL	123
AUSTRALIA	127
DARWIN	130
BACK IN-COUNTRY	132
HUE	138
BASTOGNE	143
NAPALM	150
AGENT ORANGE	152
MEDEVACKED	154
A WEEK IN THE REAR	156
BACK TO DONG HA	158
FOOTLOOSE & FANCY-FREE	161
I LOVE A PARADE	162
THE CAM LO GRAND PRIX	167
FINAL DAYS	169
BACK IN "THE WORLD"	173
A BRIEF HISTORY OF INDO CHINA	179
THOMAS WHITE	182
GLOSSARY	184

Cowards die many times before their deaths;
The valiant never taste death but once.
Of all the wonders that I yet have heard
It seems to me most strange that men should fear;
Seeing that death, a necessary end,
Will come when it will come.

William Shakespeare, *Julius Caesar*

FORT SILL - OKLAHOMA

I was drafted in early November of 1966 and was flown to Fort Lewis, Washington, for basic training in the U.S. Army. The buses loaded with the new recruits from Northern California stopped in front of Echo Company's headquarters around midnight in heavy rain. With a lot of yelling and screaming, some young sergeants wearing Smokey the Bear hats maneuvered us into a formation. As the buses drove away, we were ordered to stand at attention. When it seemed as if it couldn't rain any harder, the orderly room door opened and a really big First Sergeant came out to greet us. "Howdy boys, hope ya'll had a nice flight . . ."

Forgive me. It actually went more like this . . . "I guess you fuck-heads are starting to realize you're in the Army now. If any of you shit-for-brains thinks he can mess with me, I'll rip your fucking arm off your body and beat you over the head with it!"

He walked up and down the line studying each one of us. Someone cracked a grin and within seconds he was being held aloft by one hand and thrown to the ground. It became apparent that a carefree life, when you could break the rules once in a while, wouldn't be tolerated.

My fellow recruits standing in the rain came from all over Northern California. We were from Redding, Sacramento, and Oakland. The first friend I made on the trip to Fort Lewis was a Native American, Barney Smith, from the Hoopa Reservation north of the Trinity Alps. I was the lone inductee from Marin County, just across the Golden Gate from San Francisco. This was my introduction to a more accurate depiction of the people who make up America.

I remembered watching our country's racial unrest during the 1950s and 60s. The savage injustice displayed on our black and white TV along with my parents' wise counseling taught me the ills of this prejudice. My high school didn't have any black students, although the surrounding schools were more diverse. The only time I had rubbed elbows with an African American was when my basketball team played other schools.

By the time the buses dropped us off in the rain, I had spent enough time with these men to reaffirm my beliefs. We were all serving the same purpose—the preservation of our country, our brothers, and ourselves.

Soldier By Chance

I was lost at first, but soon considered every aspect of Basic Training a challenge, so I tried my absolute best. Six weeks later I was completely "gung-ho." On the last day, the drill sergeant who greeted us in the rain barked out our next assignment.

"Adkins, infantry! Allen, infantry! Allsworth, infantry! Anderson, infantry! Benjamin, artillery! Billings, infantry! And so it went. There was a medic and a clerk, an MP and a cook, but most were infantry. As we neared the W's, I just assumed I would remain in Fort Lewis with the future grunts in advanced infantry training.

"White, turret mechanic!"

Turret Mechanic? What the fuck?

Next day I was on a flight to the Aberdeen Proving Grounds in Maryland. The large base on the upper Chesapeake Bay is where the military developed and tested their weapons. After reporting in, a jeep took me to barracks where I would share the upper floor with my class of future turret mechanics. This group of eight was the smallest to go through the school. Our classroom was a huge warehouse with about ten weapons neatly lined up. A crane was suspended from the ceiling and ran up and down its length. It stopped above each gun as we worked our way down the line of weaponry.

The first turret we took apart was the .50-caliber machine gun on the back of a jeep. If it had a turret, we removed it, disassembled it, and put it back together. This included lifting them off the tanks and going through everything, including hydraulics, electrical components, and even replacing the gun tube.

We were tested after each different weapon, and I suppose because of the extra attention we received, all of us got high scores. Sharing the top floor of a barracks and eight-hour classes five nights a week for three months allowed us to get to know each other very well.

The class leader, Howie Johnson, was a Spec Five. He was in the National Guard and had kids at home. There was an enlistee or two, but most of us were drafted. Ray Brown, Tom Manual, and Ernie Decker were my closest friends. Our class was conducted at night and we spent a good portion of the day doing homework.

After studying every gun that floated around on ball bearings, it was time to go to work. The Army flew me to Fort Sill in Oklahoma to fulfill my 45-G30 Military Occupation Specialty

(MOS). I was now the turret mechanic for Charlie Battery, Eighth Battalion, Fourth Artillery, charged with keeping the four 175mm guns in good working order. This was the last weapon we studied in Aberdeen and the biggest.

It was a rainy night when I arrived on Vietnam Hill at Fort Sill, so named because every soldier who stood on it would deploy to Vietnam. I reported to the orderly room and stood at attention in front of the desk of First Sergeant Desmond while he read my orders.

"Private White reporting, First Sergeant."

"Ah, White. Oh-oh . . . turret mechanic, Specialist Nelson arrived this morning and took the job. Let's see . . . Corporal Horner is short a man. Report to him, three barracks down."

"Yes, First Sergeant."

June bugs covered the ground as I crunched my way to report to Corporal Horner. I had never even heard of these giant bugs that hatch once a year in the summer. They slowly buzz around and are terrible flyers, crashing into everything and falling to the ground, spending a good part of their short life trying to get airborne again. I kind of felt like one of them on my way to see the corporal, wondering where I would end up.

Sergeant Bird's gun crew occupied the bottom floor of the barracks, and before I could ask where Horner was, they pointed upstairs. Corporal Horner was a car salesman from Florida and he introduced his men with the enthusiasm of selling me a Buick. I was never hell-bent on being a mechanic, so this might not be so bad. As I was stashing my gear on an upper bunk, a big boy sauntered up to me.

"So . . . I hear you're from California."

"Afraid so."

"Christ almighty, you assholes stand out as much as the niggers."

He walked back to some of his crew and they looked my way with shit-eating grins.

Yikes! Where have I ended up!? Put me on a turret and hand me a greasy wrench! Before the Army I had rarely heard the n-word in my sheltered world. I was still reeling from all this when an even bigger guy with Westmoreland on his name tag stuck his head in my face.

"California's full of nothin' but hotrods and queers, and I don't see any hub caps on you."

That's all he said in a thick Southern drawl, as he joined his friends who were glaring at me.

Hold on to your seat, Tommy, this is going to be a bumpy ride. I was lying on the upper bunk before lights out, dreading my situation. Ruzek, the guy who first greeted me, had been staring at me from his berth.

"Hey White."

"Yeah."

"You're a lucky son of a bitch."

"I'm not feeling it at the moment . . . Why?"

Ruzek's shit-eating grin broadened.

"Well, I'll tell ya. Cosgrove and Smith left a few days ago and they were some badass boys."

"What happened to them?"

"The MPs pulled them out of here, fighting all the way . . . Don't ya wanna know why?"

I lay there silently.

"They beat a guy to death with an entrenching tool in the bunk below you. You're his replacement."

That explained why the mattress was gone.

Ruzek and his buddies chuckled and Corporal Horner yelled, "Lights Out!"

My heart raced in the dark. This was REALLY going to be a bumpy ride.

For the life of me, I don't know how I avoided getting the shit kicked out of me. These boys just flat out did not like me. I slept lightly and watched my back. This was the most difficult time I had in the Army, even more than my tour of duty in Vietnam.

Vietnam Hill was by itself on the edge of the huge artillery base. The 8th Battalion, 4th Artillery, occupied the Hill training for war before sailing overseas.

Fort Sill was originally a base for African American soldiers before the Army was desegregated after World War II. Now it was an artillery training ground.

.175-millimeter, self propelled gun

In Vietnam, our gun was the biggest cannon on the ground. The barrel was over thirty feet long and it would retract on a large track vehicle for travel. The twenty-eight-ton beast could go up to fifty miles per hour.

The consequences of a mishap with this weapon required its operation to be as simple as possible. When aligned for the range, not the distance but the area, a hydraulic blade, like on a dozer, digs in and lifts the back to level the gun and prevents the whole thing from jumping backwards when it fires. The tube is extended and she's ready to go. Each gun had a crew of eighteen. The men were assigned a specific task, starting with the driver of the ammunition carrier who delivered the 156-pound projectiles, or projos, and the 100-pound canisters of powder to the guns.

The huge self-propelled cannon also had a driver. The projo guys screw the fuse into the tip of the projectile and set the timer. These bad boys can detonate above the ground to shower shrapnel over a wide area, on impact to blow the hell out of something or penetrate bunkers underground with fuse delay. After setting the timer, they carry it to the hydraulic lift operated by the assistant gunner who slides it into the breach and locks it in with a hydraulic ram. Then the powder man hands up the right amount to push in behind the projo. Stage one, two, or three.

Most of our fire missions required three powder bags to propel the large projectiles out of sight. All three of the silk-encased powder bags weighed 100 pounds, and we rarely had a bag left over. There was an igniter on the rear of the bags signified by a red dot. The assistant gunner closes the big breach, inserts the primer and connects the lanyard, while the gunner, situated in the only seat on this thing, raises the barrel to the right azimuth. Then the assistant swings it around to the proper deflection and everyone jumps off. The gunner pulls the lanyard and KABAAM! I never saw one of these babies hit the ground in either Oklahoma or Vietnam. They just went too far, up to twenty-five miles.

It was probably a good thing that we worked so hard during the week preparing, which allowed only weekend nights at the beer hall on Vietnam Hill. One night, after having too many, I overheard this guy next to me talking about surfing and Newport Beach. I told him I surfed too, and introduced myself. He jumped up and shook my hand with a giant grin. He knew more about me than the boys on my gun did. His name was Gill Easterfeed, and apparently, he was the only Californian in Bravo Battery. Just like that, I had a new friend. Those are some crazy odds.

Acting Corporal Horner was now acting Sergeant Horner and he always acted as if he just sold you a new car. He often flashed a big grin and had a positive attitude for as long as I knew him. He accepted me as a soldier right away, not a California boy. However, some of his gun crew still wanted to throw me under the tracks of the 175.

We all trained with the M-16 for a week after they were issued to us. This was a completely different rifle than the M-14 which we spent a month shooting in basic training. Without much of a kick, it wasn't hard to qualify as expert with this weapon.

When I was ten, my Dad gave me a BB gun for Christmas. We lived on the San Francisco Bay, south of San Quentin, with millions of birds. I was a good shot and proceeded to kill quite a few of them before wounding one. I cradled the bird in my hands, looked into its eyes, and never shot another. Now we were being trained to kill men. An inner conflict was beginning to brew.

After dozens of inoculations and classes, the battalion bivouacked for a week on the huge artillery range. We rode on top of the guns to the camp and began the process of positioning them. Once the target area is established, the "Chief of Smoke," the sergeant in charge of all four guns, sets up an instrument like for surveying, with the executive officer to align the artillery pieces with a compass. Reference stakes are pounded in on the sides of the guns for their sights to adjust to. The Fire Direction Center (FDC) sends the gunner the target information over a landline and the process of firing the beast begins.

The earplugs we were issued seemed a must, but eventually they were traded in for fingers. I knew this was a big weapon, but I had no idea how big until I watched and heard it in action. *Whoa.*

My job at this time was to carry the big projectiles to the hydraulic lift with another gun bunny, set the timer on the fuse, and go back for another. In time, I could advance to delivering the powder to the assistant gunner. After proving myself to be an efficient powder deliverer, an assistant gunner's job might open up on one of the guns, and before my tour was up, I might be sitting in the gunner's seat.

This was a tough time for me. Private Westlock from the Midwest was the only man who even talked to me, aside from Horner. There was a guy named Darnby on Sergeant Davis's gun crew who went out of his way to be friendly with me, but that was it.

After training with Sergeant Horner and the boys, I decided to seek other employment, which is difficult to do in the Army. Going home to think about it wasn't an option, so I decided to volunteer for undesirable jobs. Door gunner, Radio Telegraph Operator (RTO) for Forward Observers, demolition, anything but tunnel rat. I did not want to spend the next year on the big gun.

As I was making this request to our CO, Captain Tobiason, First Lieutenant Carpenter overheard me and dug up my file with the help of Kibisky, the clerk. Carpenter was the Executive Officer (XO), the second in command of Charlie Battery. The captain was explaining that there wasn't much he could do. The lieutenant spoke to him and set my open file on his desk.

"Hmmm . . . says here you went to college for two years and something about officer candidate school."

"Yes, sir."

"We can do this for you, Private White. Report to Lieutenant McCarthy and move into the Fire Direction barracks."

"Yes, sir. Thank you, sir."

Kibisky winked at me as I walked out of the Orderly Room (OR).

Fortunately, coming from California was not a big deal with the men in FDC. I was still the odd man out and knew nothing about fire direction but was much more at ease. These guys were friendly with me, and none of them wanted to beat me to death with an entrenching tool in my sleep.

Spending the rest of my tour with these men would be considerably different from the regimen the boys on the guns would experience and the world I would have lived in. I was really lucky.

Now I was training with FDC, learning how to plot targets on topographical maps, the proper radio procedure, and how to set up the equipment on the Armored Personnel Carrier (APC). Our APC was not for transporting infantry. It was taller, with radios and the fire direction equipment, essentially the battle command center of Charlie Battery. Every man in the section displayed a lot of patience breaking me in. These were some really smart guys. I wondered what I was doing there.

Specialists Jim Kornowski and Ken Howden were our section leaders. Newly promoted E-4, Jimmy Hobbs, was third in line. Wayne Sofian was the APC driver and Richard Kellerman was our RTO. David Garfield and Owen Murphy, along with me, rounded out our crew. Second Lieutenants Bilky and McCarthy completed the FDC section.

After another week in the field, the battalion was ready to pack it up for the journey overseas. I was the low man in this group of eight who had spent their time training in artillery while I was in Maryland learning how to maintain it.

Sofian, Howden, and Hobbs in front of APC

The town of Lawton just outside of Fort Sill was other-worldly. There were three or four square blocks of beer bars crawling with a thousand soldiers from the base. On average, two or three women per block danced in the windows of the most crowded bars, causing disturbances. There were lots of disturbances. I don't think the local girls ventured near this part of town. Two visits to Lawton were enough for me. I decided to spend my nights off at the beer hall on Vietnam Hill.

I hung out with some of my FDC section and met up with Tom Manuel from Alpha Battery. Our other classmate from Aberdeen, Ray Brown, was working all the time. I don't think Ray ever picked up a wrench to work on a turret before he was promoted to be the clerk for Bravo Battery. Ernie Decker, an actual turret mechanic in Service Battery, and Westlock, joined us on weekends.

Soldier By Chance

Garfield, Hobbs, Sofian, and Kellerman

Days after I arrived at Fort Sill, First Sergeant Desmond chose me to carry the colors for our battery. After hours of drilling with Lieutenant Carpenter, I was ready to go. Just before going overseas, the base held a giant parade on the Fourth of July. Thousands marched up and down the huge parade field as all of our equipment, the guns, trucks, jeeps, and Connexes went by rail to Houston. There, they were loaded on a ship bound for Southeast Asia through the Panama Canal.

SAN FRANCISCO

The whole battalion got a week's leave right after the parade. My girlfriend, Nancy, had just sent me a Dear John letter. The kiss off. After spending a day and a half at the Dallas Fort Worth airport brooding about my lost love, I finally made it home on military standby.

As the war was escalating overseas, so was its opposition in the U.S., especially in the San Francisco Bay Area.

I spent the year before I was drafted with the Drama Department at the College of Marin, which had become a bastion of pacifism. My classmates were diligent in their endeavors to dissuade me from going to Vietnam. I believe my induction inspired them to triple their efforts to avoid following me. None of them ever did.

In an attempt to pull me out of the funk of my recent breakup with Nancy, my friends Kent and Lawrie took me to see Jimi Hendrix at the Fillmore Auditorium. I had never heard of him, although I had spent many a Friday and Saturday night at the Fillmore before I was drafted. The Jefferson Airplane, Grateful Dead, Quicksilver Messenger Service, Big Brother and the Holding Company, Steve Miller Blues Band, and the Sons of Chaplin were some of the local bands.

The moment we entered the old auditorium, it was obvious a change had taken place in the city by the bay. The colorful crowd of people bouncing to the music was now replaced by a darker, more somber group of souls who were not bouncing to the music on this night. Kent told me that there was a lot of anger about the war and a large supply of heroin was being consumed throughout the Bay Area.

The previous year, the crowd below the band could be in the hundreds. On this night, my friends and I were by ourselves in front of the "Experience." Hendrix blew our minds playing that upside down and backwards Stratocaster with a seventy-foot-high wall filled with pulsating amoebas dancing behind the three-piece band. Although he played like a madman, Jimi wasn't inspired to set his guitar on fire with lighter fluid for the three of us standing in awe below him.

Before I returned to Fort Sill, Nancy wanted to see me. We both hoped to stay friends. She lived in an apartment near the top of Twin Peaks. It looked down on Market Street all the way to the Ferry Building and the Bay Bridge crossing over to Oakland. We planned to spend the day together and she would take me to the airport the next afternoon.

A year earlier, a friend had given us two sugar cubes laced with LSD. At the time, fear kept us from consuming them and we wrapped them in tin foil and stashed them in her freezer. I loved Nancy and maybe this friend arrangement wasn't such a good idea. After staring at the refrigerator for a while, one of those sugar cubes was dissolving in my mouth. The hot afternoon summoned me outside, and before long, I was under the spell of Lysergic Acid. The vivid colors, the time-lapsed fan following all movement, the warm comforting feeling, and the clarity of the universe became overwhelming. I had to share this with Nancy. She had a doctor's appointment in the morning, but the energy emanating from me convinced her of its insignificance and soon we were tripping together.

Holding hands, we walked down to Haight Ashbury marveling at everything on the way and felt like a magic carpet took us back to her house. We talked for hours about love, war, and the cosmos, watching the full moon settle into the fog in the west as the sun rose over the Oakland Hills. It was amazing.

After more discussion and a lot of soul searching, I decided to ride this train to the end in the hope that answers would present themselves. Hiding in the woods and moving to Canada was overruled. Returning to Oklahoma and doing my best to be a good soldier while figuring this whole thing out was going to be the path for me. Nancy drove me to the airport later and the "friend'" thing had indeed worked out. I felt rejuvenated flying back to Fort Sill, ready for "Peace and Love" . . . or war.

Vietnam Hill was a completely different place when I returned from leave. All the vehicles were on their way overseas and the married men and officers had extra time for their furloughs. The hustle and bustle of a battalion preparing for war was replaced by hot and lazy dead time.

Before I flew back to Oklahoma, Nancy had given me a tinfoil packet of Orange Sunshine. LSD was legal then and Orange Sunshine was as good as you could get.

On one of the sultry days, Gil Easterfeed and I walked up to the big base pool in swimsuits and flip flops. Those bright orange pills were starting to take effect as we made our way up the hill. The day was incredibly hot, and the pool was overflowing with people. I was fascinated as I watched my friend staring at the liquid, contemplating his entry. First, a toe retracted like it never felt water before. After thirty minutes, Gil had finally made it to the center of the pool. He stood there in chest-high water as kids splashed and frolicked all around him. After immersing the entirety of his being under water, I was certain the expression on his face would draw attention, but no one seemed to notice.

We spent that blistering July day with Middle America under the influence of LSD and survived. Gil was afraid the senses the drug had heightened would be dulled from that point forward. I finally came to my senses realizing LSD was too powerful to take to war. There were a few of the orange tablets left and I flushed them.

Soon the rest of the battalion returned from leave. I looked forward to the next chapter of my journey.

The *Upshur* Band of Merry Men

U.S. NAVAL SHIP *UPSHUR*

On the day we left Fort Sill, there was an open house for friends and family. Chaplains blessed the battalion and before noon we were flying to Tacoma, Washington. We boarded the Navy troop ship, the USNS *Upshur*, and in a couple of hours, she was underway. Hundreds of hammocks stacked two-high filled each of the large holds. I secured my equipment on one of them and went topside for the sail out of Puget Sound. The ship passed through the Strait of Juan de Fuca at dusk as we left the U.S. for the open sea. Many of my shipmates had never seen the ocean. It was surprising how quickly the novelty had worn off as they drifted below. I was alone on deck as we chased the sun until our homeland disappeared in the night.

Sailing across the Pacific on the *Upshur* was almost like a three-week vacation from the Army. For me, anyway. It also counted as time spent overseas.

Weather permitting, calisthenics were mandatory on the foredeck each morning. We had to salute officers outside, which wasn't often because most of them stayed on the upper decks. The rest of our time was spent eating, sleeping, or roaming around where we could on the ship. At night, two large rooms hosted movies with more than a hundred men attending each showing. Most of my fellow passengers were bored out of their minds on this voyage, but you put me anywhere on the water, and it's all good.

One morning the captain of the ship summoned me to the bridge. It turns out my mother went to the University of California at Berkeley with Captain Rhodes. They still stayed in touch, explaining how he knew I was on board. He sat me down and we talked about my mom. I got the feeling Captain Rhodes had the hots for her over twenty years ago. We shook hands, saluted, and he told me to come up anytime, and I did.

I was the artist on the daily mimeographed newspaper that a handful of us published each day. Gil Easterfeed got me the job. Our little newspaper office was on the upper deck where the officers and the non-commissioned officers slept and ate. We got the latest news from a daily news wire and put out our little paper. I laid it out and drew cartoons about a GI named Charlie meeting Charlie the VC. Cute and very naïve. We ate upstairs in the officers' mess for most of our meals at the Merchant Marine table. The *Upshur* was a Navy ship with navy officers, but the crew were Merchant Marines.

Soldier By Chance

Original illustration from the *Upshur Newsletter* by Thomas White

I made friends with some of the Merchant Marines in the dining room. They invited me to watch the rotating movie with them in their dayroom instead of the hot crowded smoke-filled rooms below. The best part of this friendship was hanging out with them on the fantail. The upper decks blocked a lot of the wind and the spray from the bow slicing through the sea, a mist that rarely made its way that far astern. There was a large foredeck on the bow where the men in the holds were allowed to escape the heat below, and the NCOs and officers had the upper decks to get their dose of fresh air. The Navy crew and the Merchant Marines shared the most ideal place above deck on the *Upshur*; the fantail. I ended up sleeping out there most of the time. The cooks would throw the garbage over the side to the delight of the Albatross that floated behind us. The sunsets were incredible, followed by the plankton-enriched sea frothing bright white in the ship's wake at night. Dolphins gliding in and out of the water beside us helped make this voyage anything but boring.

As far as I was concerned, this time at sea was a huge bonus. There were some complaints about the chow, but I thought the Navy food was better than ours. My Fire Direction section got to know each other without an officer breathing down our necks. We had no duty or fire missions. I didn't consider my time with the newspaper a chore, as it gave me something to do. In this brief casual atmosphere, some friendships had time to grow. Manual, Brown, and Decker were already buddies from Aberdeen. Hobbs and Garfield in FDC were fast becoming friends. This was the only time that Kibisky wouldn't be behind a desk with a stack of paperwork and land line phones ringing. The Merchant Marines had a lot of time off and a few of them joined our band of Merry Men, along with Westlock.

I loved surfing or sailing in stormy seas and hoped the *Upshur* would encounter some. My wish came true in the middle of the Pacific when we hit a wild storm head-on. The hallways were lined with men sitting or leaning against the walls, filling the walkways with vomit. The bathrooms were unreachable, and if you did, there was no going in.

I grew up sailing on the San Francisco Bay and had some sea legs. After maneuvering through the maze of pale green men lining the hallway, I made it to the galley with a few others. The galley went beam to beam, the whole width of the ship with portholes on the sides. When she was in mid-tilt, there was a sea of slop on the floor of syrup, milk, mushed up goop, and barf. As it would roll to the side, a foot of this mixture would surge against the wall like a crashing wave. After managing to eat, I tried to time my departure with the tide of slop. But I misjudged and twenty feet from the side, I surfed the wave with my stainless-steel mess tray

Soldier By Chance

held in front of me, slamming against the wall, just barely able to stay upright, escaping an impossible task of ridding myself of the goop. Not long after this, my gastronomic superiority failed me and I expelled my breakfast somewhere on the ship to mix with the sea sloshing about below decks.

    I went up on the foredeck to ride out the storm for a while and to escape the stale air fermenting below. The bow would bury itself in the surging sea sending mountains of spray to blend with torrential rainfall. I stayed up there long after dark under some cover. A series of intense lightning strikes lit up the violent ocean for moments on end as the old ship rocked and rolled through the storm.

Tom White aboard the *Upshur*

I have bedimm'd the noontide sun,
Called forth the mutinous winds
And twixt the green sea and the azured vault
Set roaring war: to the dread rattling thunder
Have I given fire.

      William Shakespeare *The Tempest*

OKINAWA

The shipload of troops got one six-hour shore leave on Okinawa. We docked at Whites Bay with a Vegas-styled playground close by for those who wanted to go ashore. The *Upshur* was empty in no time. The casino was huge with slot machines, gaming tables, bars, and local girls dancing in bikinis on platforms or in cages hanging from the ceiling.

I stood at the entrance gazing in for a while and decided to go AWOL (Absent Without Leave). I hitched a ride in the back of a pickup for a few miles on this barren part of the island, when we came to a hill where I could see in the distance and realized my quest was a futile one. The very friendly family in the old truck let me out and I walked back to the ship.

I should have known better. Okinawa is a big island. During World War Two it took months to secure and the U.S. lost over 12,000 soldiers before the few surviving Japanese surrendered. Their casualties were enormous, with over 100,000 killed. Estimates place the loss of life among Okinawa civilians between 40,000 and 150,00 people; nearly one-third of the population. Hopefully, history will prove it was the last battle of its kind.

My father had three brothers. The oldest, Jack, was an Army artillery man wounded on D-Day in Normandy. He never fully recovered. Bill was a Navy Yeoman who yearned to be in the submarine service. He left a sub tender on Midway to join the crew of the USNS *Wahoo* on her last voyage. The decorated submarine went down with all hands in the waters off Northern Japan. My dad, George White, was a B-24 Navigator guiding fifty missions through "The Slot" in the Pacific. He earned the Distinguished Flying Cross with two oak leaf clusters. His twin brother, my namesake Tom, was a first lieutenant in the Marines storming the beach on Tinian, Iwo Jima, and Okinawa where he was killed. After learning there was a large cemetery close by, but not that close, I thought I might find his grave. As it turned out, all of our losses on Okinawa had come home to their final resting place.

The rest of the voyage was spent in unrelenting heat, easily over a hundred degrees with stifling humidity. We passed to the west of the Philippines just close enough to see the image of their shore as the ship closed in on our home for the coming year.

Jack Alexander White (uncle)　　　William Thomas White (uncle)

Thomas George White (uncle)　　　George Thomas White (father)

D - DAY

Early morning starlight glittered on the calm water as the *Upshur* neared the shores of Vietnam. The South China Sea gently lapped against her as she plowed through the sultry darkness. After three weeks at sea, the aging ship's collection of sounds had merged into one that almost disappeared.

I was on the bow knowing that the end of our voyage was at hand with the smell of land reaching us, without a breath of air to deliver it. Sleeping wasn't easy in the cargo holds filled with hundreds of hammocks stacked two-high. They were covered, so the stale air along with the intensified heat made the big rooms uncomfortable. If it was ninety degrees outside, the temperature down below was over a hundred. I slept on deck when the weather allowed it. More often than not, the upper decks were empty at night, but on this particular early morning, the anticipation of landfall brought a crowd topside to witness its sighting.

And there it was . . . an illumination round anyway, and then another. This was the first sign we were entering a war-torn country where darkness was at a premium for the enemy. This illumination of the night would follow us throughout our travels in Vietnam.

The ship slowly entered Da Nang Harbor on a sheet of black glass. The only sound penetrating the old ship's halting moan was the hissing of an illumination round slowly drifting earthward and the occasional pop of a new one coming to life. Five or so orange glows were spread out above the mountains surrounding the bay, their cumulative light casting enough radiance to see them silhouetted behind the city. Da Nang was a network of shadows along the waterfront. It was pitch black. The only light emanated from the flares above the hills.

The 8th Battalion, 4th Artillery, in its entirety, was waiting on deck when the anchor splashed into the warm water. We carried a big canvas duffle bag filled with everything necessary for the next year, along with all the personal items you could stuff in it. Our stateside uniforms that would gladly be exchanged later for the clothes designed for this climate were wet from perspiration brought on by our nervous energy and the intense predawn heat.

Each of us must have been absorbed in thought, for no one spoke. Some couldn't get off the ship fast enough, while there were those who would have preferred to stay on board. I remember being wide-eyed without a clue about where we were going or what would befall us in the upcoming year.

We were crammed together waiting to climb down the rope webbing hanging from the side to the landing craft when the sun finally inched its way above the dark blue horizon casting enough light for a safe departure. This was not a secure area, so all of us had been issued a basic load of ammunition for our M-16s. The battalion's combat time had begun paying me one hundred dollars extra a month, more for the higher ranks. First Lieutenant Carpenter was in front about to issue the order to disembark when he saw my helmet. "What the Hell is that!? Am I seeing things? Fucking A, Westlock, you, too?"

"It's a peace sign, sir," I replied. Lieutenant Carpenter was a little agitated as he turned pink and ordered us to remove them. I had just inked them on the front of our helmet covers the previous night. Private Westlock unstrapped his bayonet and cut the symbol of the anti-war movement escalating back home free of his helmet, while I blackened mine in to form a big dot. Westlock, the Indiana farm boy on Horner's gun, didn't care where I was from. He was the only friend I had in the early days at Fort Sill. Peace signs removed, we slung our rifles and dropped the bags down to waiting hands bobbing in the boats below. The landing craft engines and the clamor of our M-16s made the only noise as we climbed down the webbing and motored to shore. A very peaceful D-Day.

Most Army Battalions are comprised of companies with platoons. An Artillery Battalion has batteries with gun crews. The battalion with Charlie Battery moved not far off the beach to unload the Connexes, big steel shipping containers full of everything a 175 battery would need, right down to First Sergeant Desmond's steel desk. How many times you stood at attention in front of it depended on you.

Each of the four .175mm self-propelled guns that C-Battery was all about were supported by a three-quarter-ton truck and a tracked M548 ammunition carrier. The officers and NCOs had jeeps to cart them around and FDC relied on an APC command track, the M577. Motor pool provided deuce-and-a-half and 5-ton trucks to supply the big guns with ammunition and Charlie Battery with provisions.

All of these vehicles and the Connexes preceded us, also by ship, and were waiting when the 8th and the 4th hit the beach in Da Nang. The guns that we were here to support sat on two large landing craft waiting for their voyage up the coast.

We were issued flak jackets and canvas and leather boots to replace our black shiny clunkers. They had a tin plate on the bottom between the soles for punji stake protection. A year later, the steel plates had broken into pieces and rattled around the bottom of my boots. They were worn out, but fit like a glove.

As we prepared for our first mission, we soon learned it was a convoy or land march to Dong Ha in the North. Our big guns were too heavy to cross some of the bridges on Highway 1. The Navy would transport them up the coast to Dong Ha.

I had a few opportunities to ride through the streets of Da Nang on supply runs. Like the attitude of "Fuck the Army" or FTA, another ugly trend reared its head in Vietnam.

I was fascinated by this place as we drove through town. On one of the side streets, we passed a beautiful Vietnamese woman dressed in a white silk jacket and the black silk pants almost everyone wore. She stopped on the road and slid one of her pants legs up and over her gorgeous butt. Her long black hair almost covered it, while she squatted and took a shit as we drove by. I must admit to being surprised by this, and as we drove along, I was surprised a lot. This scene was too much for some of the other volunteers. On the next run for supplies, an attitude adjustment had taken place. The soldiers were now shouting obscenities to people on the street and "boom, boom" to the woman. I was uncomfortable with this but kept my mouth shut. This was going to be a strange war.

We unpacked the Connexes and Motor Pool prepared the vehicles for the convoy. While all of this was going on, Bravo Battery was already with the First Marine Division at Camp Brooks. They would stay close to Da Nang for more than a year. I never saw those guys again.

Before dawn, in August, Alpha, Charlie, Service, and Headquarters (HQ) batteries were lined up and ready for the one-hundred-mile trip to Dong Ha.

I was sitting on top of the APC when Staff Sergeant Breem, the Chief of Smoke, was calling out for a volunteer to escort and drive the four 175s off the Landing Craft at our destination in Dong Ha. Breem was the NCO in charge of all four guns. Apparently, none of the drivers wanted to go to sea again. I grabbed my gear, leapt to the ground, jumped into a jeep, and was driven to the docks as the sun crested above the South China Sea.

The large convoy rolled out for the hundred-mile ride to Dong Ha. Their orders were to exhibit a "show of force," driving through the centers of Phu Bai, Hue, and Quang Tri.

Da Nang Street Scene - Capital, Quang Nam–Da Nang Province

DONG HA

After three days on land, I found myself back onboard ship with the Navy. It was over a hundred degrees when the two Landing Craft (LST) left the harbor and skirted the coast out of small arms range. By midday, the temperature had dropped considerably as we plowed through the sea heading north.

For now, all I had to do was enjoy the voyage as well as the Navy's food. The LST had its own galley with everything including a well-stocked refrigerator, an appliance we would see little of. This one had fresh eggs, bacon, milk, right down to steaks in the freezer.

After the last of three hearty meals, I rolled out my sleeping bag on the deck and watched the sun set behind the mysterious mountains in Laos as misty clouds crept towards us from the sea. When daylight evaporated into darkness, there were stretches along the coast that were pitch black—a rare sight as illumination rounds would follow us almost everywhere.

When day broke, it was cold and damp. So was I.

One hundred yards offshore, fishermen were spread out in long boats tied to bamboo poles imbedded in the sandy bottom. The stiff on-shore wind pointed them all toward the beach. Some ignored us, while others kept waving until we disappeared in the mist.

By early afternoon, we approached the Cau Viet River and followed it ten miles west to Dong Ha. What started out as a drizzly day was becoming a rainy one and the wind was stronger as it barreled down from the north with a cold bite to it. The big LSTs beached along the riverbank in front of town by the Highway 1 bridge. I was along on this voyage to drive the guns off the landing craft. Most of us had licenses to drive all the vehicles, but the convoy had arrived earlier, so each driver was waiting to take his gun back to camp. I rode with Sergeant Bird on his 175. He personally wanted to drive his baby to our new base. Back in Oklahoma, Bird had accepted me right away. I really liked the man and our friendship would grow in the coming months.

Bridge at Dong Ha with US Navy landing craft docked on opposite shore

Alpha's four guns would arrive in a few days after the LSTs returned with them. A-Battery would then move to Camp Carroll. Service and HQ Batteries set up on the west edge of the Third Marine Division fire base at Dong Ha. C-Battery was based a hundred meters to the north. We were positioned so our 175s wouldn't fire over our camp or nearby installations. The Navy Seabees had bulldozed pads for the guns, leveled a big area for us, and cleared a perimeter for our defenses. Butting up to the Marine base left only two sides for us to defend.

Arriving the night before, the men had quickly strung a layer of concertina wire and piled sandbags around four M-60 machine guns. By the time I got there, another layer of wire was in place with mines between them. The camp was somewhat chaotic with over a hundred men moving into position. Lieutenant McCarthy, one of the two officers in FDC, found me and I was back at work with my section.

Apparently, Hue was the highlight of the convoy. Kornowski, one of the big brains in fire direction, could not stop talking about it. They wanted to know about my voyage, but the Navy food impressed them the most. The steaks and bacon were much more interesting than my description of the sunset.

We worked until dark getting ready for fire missions. Our vehicle had lights inside, but outside the darkness enveloped everything. The only light came from the illumination rounds slowly falling to earth outside the perimeter.

It rained like crazy that first night and the newly churned earth quickly turned to red mud. We slept under the vehicles or out in the rain beneath our ponchos. The next morning C-Battery suffered its first casualty. One of our men asleep under a five-ton was run over and killed. The truck driver was never the same and wasn't with us long.

By the next day, FDC was in place and the guns were pointed towards their targets launching 156-pound projectiles across the DMZ into North Vietnam.

Tom lugs a 156-pound 'projo'

FIRING SEQUENCE FOR .175-MM GUN

Round fired - time to reload

Sergeant Bird jumps onto the gun

Dropping the tube and lowering the projo lift

Hoisting 'projo' onto lift and opening the breach

'Projo' is rammed into the open breach

Loading one-hundred pounds of powder and closing the breach

Raise the tube, aim, jump off, and fire

By the time the twenty-eight-ton track vehicles jockeyed the guns into position, even deeper mud holes were created. Following protocol, the crew would jump off the gun before pulling the lanyard. They had never fired a 175 in the mud before and it took them a while to judge the right distance to avoid getting completely splattered by it.

Before long, three rows of concertina wire and more mines covered our exposed flanks. The M-60s were dug in and surrounded by layers of sandbags and tents sheltered us from the rain. Eventually wooden frames and floors would replace the rope rigging holding them up. This made it much easier, of course, to stack more sandbags around them. They still leaked, however, but only a few complained. We knew a lot of our guys out there had no cover for days on end.

As our guns kept firing, the wooden boxes holding the powder had accumulated. Inside was a thick steel container to protect the one hundred pounds of powder necessary to propel the big projectiles twenty-five miles away. We filled these canisters inside the crates with dirt, stacked them around everything, and covered the walls with layers and layers of sandbags.

The 105s fired a projectile that was attached to a brass powder casing. Each wooden box with rope handles held two of them and the crates were plentiful. They were easy to stack when filled with dirt, and made the best walls. An old-fashioned steam-powered trencher with buckets on a big wheel dug three, five-foot-deep trenches fifty-feet long, that we covered with the ammo boxes and layers and layers of, what else? Sandbags. This method of protection would never be used again. The first time I ducked into one was the last. I'm claustrophobic and once inside the narrow trench with other men, you were trapped. Even a small round close to the edge would collapse the sides, burying you, contributing to my decision to stay out of them. I chose to hunker down in the APC with its sandbagged protection, or if it was too far, I'd just hit the dirt. It was a crapshoot anyway, as there weren't enough sandbags to protect anything from a direct hit.

Fire Direction had an APC command vehicle like the armored personnel carriers, but taller. There was a generator up top with a small crane to lower it to the ground, radios inside with various slide rules, charts, maps, and workspaces. Once in place, the tall radio antenna opens up and is secured by guy wires. A long tent unfurls off the back and under this cover our map tables are set up. Two of us plotted the targets to ensure accuracy. The ammo boxes would make a five-foot wall around our command center and tent, which of course we covered with tons of, oh yeah. You got it. Sandbags.

Fire Direction APC command vehicle

About this time our stateside uniforms were traded for the lighter, more loose-fitting and breathable clothes designed for this climate, with black insignias and name tags.

Our opening week in Dong Ha was uneventful. The gun crews were busy shooting into or over the DMZ, which meant we were also hard at work, but it was a peaceful introduction to the Vietnam War for Charlie Battery. Between fire missions I often wondered what it was like to be on the receiving end of our artillery. I wouldn't have to wonder for long.

One afternoon when the radio squawked with incoming warnings, our introduction to fear was comical. The first line of defense at this point was a four-foot-deep hole we dug surrounded by sandbags. The wall around the tent wasn't there yet, so we dove into the hole along with Lieutenant McCarthy and the off-duty crew who had run over from the sleeping quarters. All of us wriggled around like worms trying to squeeze into the dirt. We waited . . . and waited. Kornowski and McCarthy were the first to pop their heads up. Kellerman, who remained in the APC to man the radio, ran out to tell everyone that it was a false alarm.

Cook, Sofian, Tom White, Garfield, and Hobbs

A few days later, I was leaning on our sandbag wall that went up lickety-split, gazing at the mountains in Laos, when the first enemy visitor came screaming in. *Holy shit!* The tranquil spell I was in was shattered as another landed fifty yards behind it and eight more whistled overhead to hit headquarters and service batteries. Another barrage hit the Marine firebase next to us. The two I witnessed landed in an open area fifty yards in front of me. There was a bright orange flash with dirt and shiny shrapnel exploding outward. Then came the sounds. There was a screaming whistle on their way in, the blast of the deep explosion you can feel in your bones, and the shrapnel and rocks hissing by. After crawling under a rock with a mere warning days earlier, when the real thing happened so quickly, I didn't even spill my coffee. Our battalion suffered more casualties when two men from Service Battery were killed.

Garfield, Kellerman, McCarthy, Murphy and Tom White

The main targets of this attack were the ammo and fuel dumps next door in the Marine base. We heard the .122mm rockets that blew up the supply of 175 ammunition. After a few days, our ammo was gone and until the C-130's could resupply us, the four guns were quiet. More time to fill sandbags. The guns were priority one, so it wasn't long before the big planes replenished Charlie Battery's reason for being there.

We were working our butts off, averaging around four hours sleep, and after one month in Dong Ha, the base was taking shape. Motor Pool's big Quonset hut was up covering the vast array of tools and equipment it took to keep all of the vehicles and the guns online. Service Battery, next door for the moment, really had serious machinery that could fix or rebuild anything. Service and Headquarters never left the base at Dong Ha, but the three gun batteries moved around following the enemy.

From a letter sent home:

> *There are only eight in FDC plus the two fire direction officers. I seldom get a chance to speak to the other shift. Hello, goodbye, as we change. The five of us are together constantly, share the same foxhole, and fill the same sandbags. We get along very well but our world is pretty small.*

Alpha Battery was long gone. When their guns arrived by sea right after ours, they left for Camp Carroll to the west of us. A Navy Seabee dozer dug a pit for our future fire command bunker. Then 12 x 12 posts and beams and the rest of the material was dropped off and we went to work.

The off-duty crew and some men from the guns, along with Broheim, our master carpenter, started cutting and banging away on it. Broheim had just finished building the wooden frames for every tent in our compound. The rains didn't cooperate, naturally, and we had to spend a day here and there with a bucket brigade to remove mud from the pit. After the crew managed to drop a big beam on me, which broke a few ribs, our medic slapped tape around my chest and called it good.

At that time, FDC was in the middle of everything, just below the mess tent and above the four guns. The orderly room and barracks were behind us. The sandbag wall in front of our tent became a meeting place. When it wasn't raining, mess kits covered the top of it during meals. The on-duty crew was on the inside, and at one time or another, almost everyone in the battery had something to say over that wall.

We had spent a few months in Oklahoma and some time at sea together. Most of our men were now leaving the bullshit behind and showing their true selves. We tended to act a little differently without any women around.

Duty in Fire Direction was the easiest part of the day. Let me rephrase that, the easiest part of the night. If your shift was during the day, you could count on shoveling sand or dirt into or onto something between fire missions.

Soldier By Chance

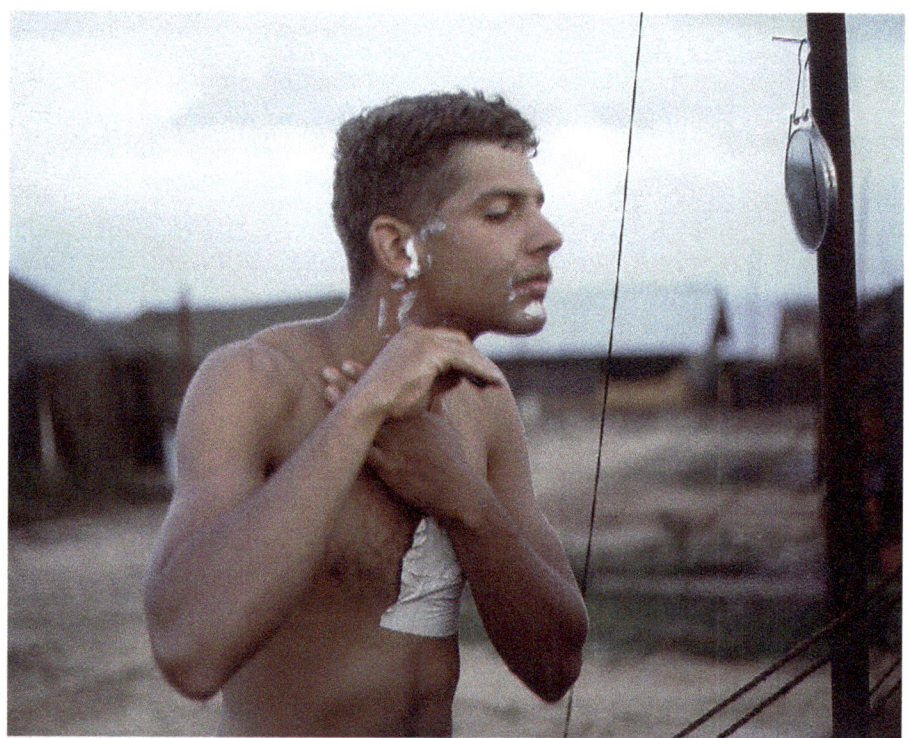
Tom with taped ribs

    After dark, if the guns were quiet, there wasn't much to do. Information from weather balloons over the radio required twenty minutes of math three or four times a day called a MET (Meteorological Information for Target Calculation). This supplied us with the wind speed, temperature, and barometric pressure at different elevations. We rotated this task between us. Occasionally, the lieutenant always by our side would take a turn. The radio telegraph operator managed the radios and the tall antenna on the APC. Two men waited at the map tables for fire missions from a Forward Observer (FO) over the radio. Once the target is plotted from the FO's coordinates, the direction, distance, and elevation are relayed to the man at the desk with the slide rules. This man then calculates the compiled information with the atmospheric data from the MET and sends the guns the azimuth and deflection, the up and down, and side to side position of the gun barrel. I started out plotting targets at the map tables and gradually learned every job in Fire Direction.

Westlock, Hobbs, Tom White, and Sofian

Some of our night missions were H & I's - Harassment and Interdiction. These were random fire missions in the middle of nowhere just in case the NVA were there. The Marine and South Vietnamese patrols relayed their locations to us to keep from getting the ultimate surprise. Friendly fire. We also supported these patrols. Some missions helped suppress ambushes, while others aided our infantry when they were the attackers. It wasn't often FDC sent the gun crews information requiring one bag of powder and elevating the gun barrel like a Howitzer.

We would have been shocked to know, as I found out just recently, that the 175 wasn't very accurate in this mode. Occasionally, it could be off by a hundred meters from one round to the next with the same azimuth and deflection. *Yikes*. The Forward Observers didn't call for incoming too close to themselves or our infantry. Good thing they knew this.

In the midst of all this, I continued reading the *Complete Works of William Shakespeare* I'd been packing with me all along, as well as a lot of other books that got passed around. Willie was never requested by anyone.

My section didn't have KP, which was an all-day affair. We did have rotating guard duty. Every week or so, two guys from my section would spend the night behind one of our M-60s spread out on the perimeter. By now the machine-gun nests were substantial. Big enough for three or four men and covered and surrounded by layers and layers of sandbags. The off-duty FDC shift would send two guys to man the nest.

There were stretches of time filled with monotony when incoming subsided and our fire missions didn't accomplish much. Lt. McCarthy, the good leader that he was, rotated our duty from 12-on, 12-off, to 8-on, 8-off. He also switched our crew members around so we got used to working with one another. Spending the night behind an M-60, peering into the darkness between the illumination rounds with these guys, strengthened our bonds. Speaking softly, our conversations revealed about everything we knew, or thought we knew. You could count on spending a quiet evening staring into the night if Howden was your partner. He wasn't much of a conversationalist, but you could rest easy because he had great night vision.

I never saw anyone to shoot at, but Kornowski and Hobbs opened up with the other nests on the northwest side during one of their shifts. A group of enemy Sappers managed to cut their way through the concertina. It wasn't until one stepped on a mine that they were noticed and cut down in short order on their way to our 175s.

We also shared a turn at latrine detail. It sounds shitty, but it was one of the easier tasks required of us. The cut in half 55-gallon drums with handles are pulled out of the outhouse from the back. The recent deposits float in diesel fuel that is set ablaze with a lit piece of toilet paper. After thirty minutes, the drums are empty and cool enough to pour in a few inches of diesel that will burn the following day. On calm days, we knew where some of the other fire bases were by the thin column of black smoke created by this early morning detail. Not a bad assignment standing around bullshitting, waiting for crap to burn.

Infrequent mortar attacks came from Viet Cong or North Vietnamese Army Regulars (NVA) fairly close by, sneaking around in the bushy draws. We had a fifty-foot-tall lookout tower, compliments of the Navy Seabees, to spot these random attackers. Butting up to a large Marine firebase with open land on the other side discouraged ground attacks, so for now, we just had to deal with these sneaky bastards in the brush. For them, this was risky business.

The incoming we received this close to the DMZ came from North Vietnam. On average, ten of the big rounds landed inside the large firebase throughout the day, most likely coming from one gun dug in somewhere trying to catch us off guard. We got used to this guy and didn't even dive for cover after a while. There were three types of Russian artillery pieces that were capable of reaching us. Trucks carrying their ammunition pulled the big guns around at night to set up under cover, spread their outriggers, and position themselves for us or someone else in their sights. They weren't as big, but had a greater range than our guns and could be deeper into North Vietnam and still reach us.

Once it started raining at Dong Ha, it did so for weeks on end. We had the early morning formation before breakfast under our ponchos and pretty much lived beneath them. By the time you waited in line for chow, or got to work, your lower half was drenched, and I wouldn't call the other half dry. All of this was a walk in the park on a Sunday afternoon compared to the wet and muddy world of the gun crews. They had no cover to escape the incessant rain. The muddy area around each 175 expanded every day as more ammo was delivered and carried to the big guns. It seemed as if every time one fired, the gun sank a little deeper into the red mud.

Jimmy Hobbs readies for guard duty

Soldier By Chance

Sergeant Bird (center) at the helm of the 175 at Dong Ha

CHINA BEACH

Our section was hard at work digging the mud out of the pit for the bunker. The fortress was coming together, but rain played havoc on our progress. One morning Kibisky climbed down the ladder into the muddy hole where we were working.

"Hey, White. Do you want to get out of here?"

"Hell no! Why would I want to do that?"

"Quit dickin' around and get cleaned up. China Beach awaits you. Meet me in the OR."

I flew up the ladder and landed in a clean uniform. Kibisky gave me a ride to the Dong Ha air base in Sergeant Desmond's jeep and I was airborne on a C-130 bound for Da Nang. Everyone got two mini-vacations during their tour. One for five days in an exotic land nearby and another with a three-day break in one of the four military zones dividing Vietnam. The soldiers in the north, I-Corps, spent their in-country Rest and Recuperation (R&R) at China Beach outside Da Nang. The beautiful resort built by the French with classic white buildings was beside a beach like many back home. Picture a lifeguard tower with a surfboard leaning against it, white sand, and waves. Everything but girls in bikinis, girls in anything. The sunny days without rain almost made up for their absence.

My first day there, I looked up at the lifeguard leaning back in his chair and asked if I could borrow his surfboard.

"Sorry, Dude, no way."

"Come on man, I've been surfing since I was 14."

"Can't do it, Bub."

While walking away, I turned and asked the guy in the tower. "Are you in the Marines?"

"No way. Army. Special forces."

I left, wondering how I hadn't thought of that. What a way to spend your year in Vietnam. He was probably RA, Regular Army. When you sign up for three years, if you're lucky, you can pick your duty.

After dinner the first night, beer flowed freely as two Dallas Cowboy cheerleaders lip-synced to "Mustang Sally" and danced. It was lame as hell, but a hundred of us went nuts, beered up, and ready to rock.

When we weren't lounging at the beach, Da Nang was nearby. This was a fascinating city. Small shops on the back streets sold everything from weapons, to drugs, and women. A man in one of the stalls engraved "Flower Man" and some daisies on my Zippo lighter before this short break was over. I felt left out missing the Summer of Love that was taking place back in "the world." Every time I heard the song on the radio about going to San Francisco and wearing some flowers in your hair, my emotions would get the best of me.

I made a friend while whistling at the cheerleaders. Sam Ozerbeck was a Marine supply Sergeant in Dong Ha. We rode back in the C-130 together and before I returned to my base, he outfitted me with a rain suit, top, and pants. In conjunction with my poncho, it was now possible to stay dry. *Possible*. He also gave me a wool overcoat liner and Marine flak jacket. I wore that flak jacket from then on. With hard clunky plates, it was an older version than ours and probably wasn't as protective, but "when in Rome." The overcoat liner would be appreciated later when the climate cooled.

QUANG TRI

Tom White, Adams, Hobbs, Murphy, Kellerman, Westlock, Kornowski, and Sofian at Dong Ha

I was back from the beach retreat and hard at work on the bunker when Captain Tobiason peered over the edge of the pit and told us we would be moving out soon and could halt construction. It wasn't often you were ordered to stop working. This also meant the bundles of sandbags could stay put for the time being. The North Vietnamese artillery was still a hindrance without any serious damage—to us, anyway, although we were often targeted because of our guns. Dong Ha was a big base and we were on the outer edge of it. The situation inside the firebase wasn't relayed to us. Throughout the year, we hardly knew anything about what was going on with the war around us.

Soldier By Chance

After seven weeks in-country, the battery packed up and moved south. We stacked more sandbags around the top edge of the APC to protect the crew who would ride up there. They also made a nice seat so you could lean back and enjoy the view. I was riding on top along with Jimmy Hobbs from Michigan. Jimmy didn't talk about his past very much, but implied he escaped some trouble back home by joining the Army. David Garfield was from Fort Worth. He was a laid-back Texan who proved to be a calming factor in our section. He was also the jokester. Jim Kornowski had a  thick Wisconsin accent and was always smiling and talking about food. He loved piping hot coffee claiming it cooled him down even when it was 120 degrees. This remedy never worked for me. Another Texan, Second Lieutenant McCarthy, also rode on top. Riding with us instead of in the jeep with the other officers said it all. McCarthy was not your conventional officer. He brought a Martin guitar with him and played it well.

Our other officer, Lieutenant Bilkey, rode in McCreedy's jeep. Second Lieutenant McCreedy was the officer overseeing the four guns with the Chief of Smoke, Staff Sgt. Breem. Bilky was a little stiff, operating 100% "by the book," but he was a good officer. I was glad McCarthy was the lieutenant on my shift most of the time. He could get down to business, but loved to horse around and play the guitar. And for a couple of bucks he'd cut our hair.

Wayne Sofian, from Detroit, was our driver. He not only drove the rig, but maintained it and the generator. He also pulled shifts in FDC. Wayne had a local bar he and his wife frequented. After a while, I could picture this place and the people in it. Kellerman 'The Rat' was our RTO, and along with another Texan from Dallas, Murphy, rode inside. The Rat and Murphy talked about their wives who they missed so much, I was tired of hearing about it and a little jealous. Howden from Michigan also rode inside. He and Kornowski were the senior members of our section along with Hobbs. Howden was also married, but said little about his life in "the world." He had a great laugh but was usually a very quiet man.

Kellerman was trained as an RTO, while the rest of FDC studied artillery fire direction at Fort Sill along with our two lieutenants who went to Officer Candidate School there. We always had an officer on duty. If one of those 156-pounders strayed, someone higher than one of us had to be accountable. Mostly draftees, we were a young group of men. I was twenty and no one topped twenty-five, including the officers. In the months to come, we would all be able to perform any of the duties in Fire Direction. However, there was no one like Kellerman on the radio, and Howden and Kornowski were the fastest with the slide rules. They were really smart men.

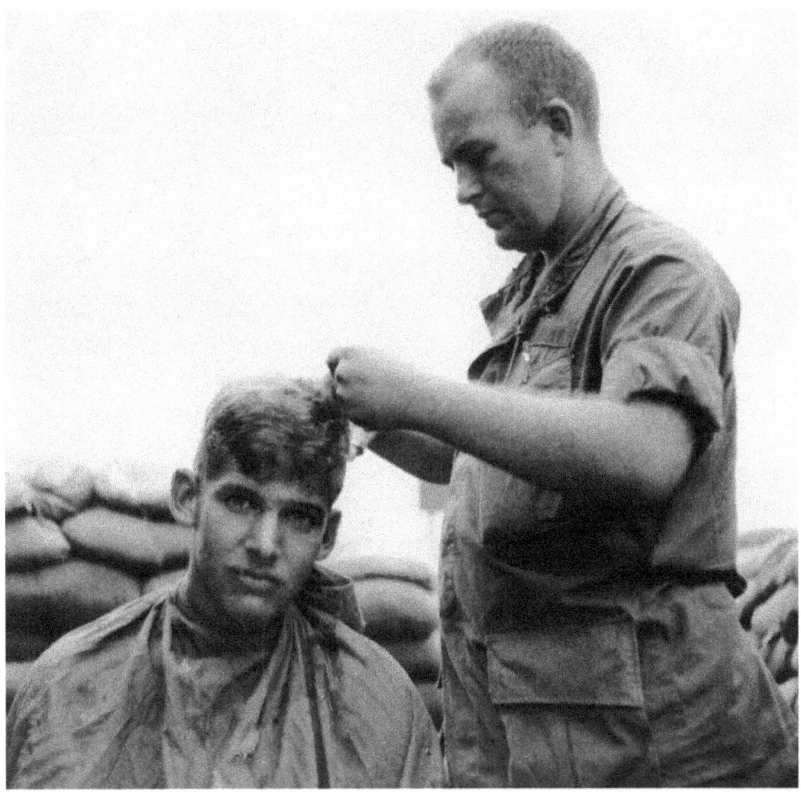

Our barber, Lieutenant McCarthy

Soldier By Chance

Heading south on Highway 1 towards Quang Tri

When it was time to leave Dong Ha, our convoy left the gates and turned onto Highway 1. The battalion had driven through here on their land march from Da Nang while I was at sea with the guns. After the junction with Highway 9 that led to Cam Lo and Camp Carroll, Charlie Battery headed south for ten miles. Small villages lined the road and rice paddies filled every flat valley. Honda-50 motorbikes, small buses, and water buffalo crowded the thoroughfare, along with a constant parade of jeeps and trucks. People just walking or carrying their burden under the yokes so many used, also mingled with the flow. In time, the lush countryside opened up to a vast sandy plain and the traffic thinned out considerably. We set up camp not far from Highway 1 on the outskirts of Quang Tri, next to an Army self-propelled 105 battery. The road continued south through the sand to infinity.

We were out of range from the enemy's big guns, so protection from them was not an issue. There were mortar attacks. They seemed like firecrackers compared to the artillery in the North, but in reality, they were very deadly. All we could see was sand and we only filled enough bags to protect the powder and build machine gun nests for guard duty. The sides of the tents were rolled up, which helped with the heat if there was a breeze. My eyes never did adjust to the bright sun bouncing off the pure white sand. When not on duty, we spent a lot of time sweating in our cots under the shade.

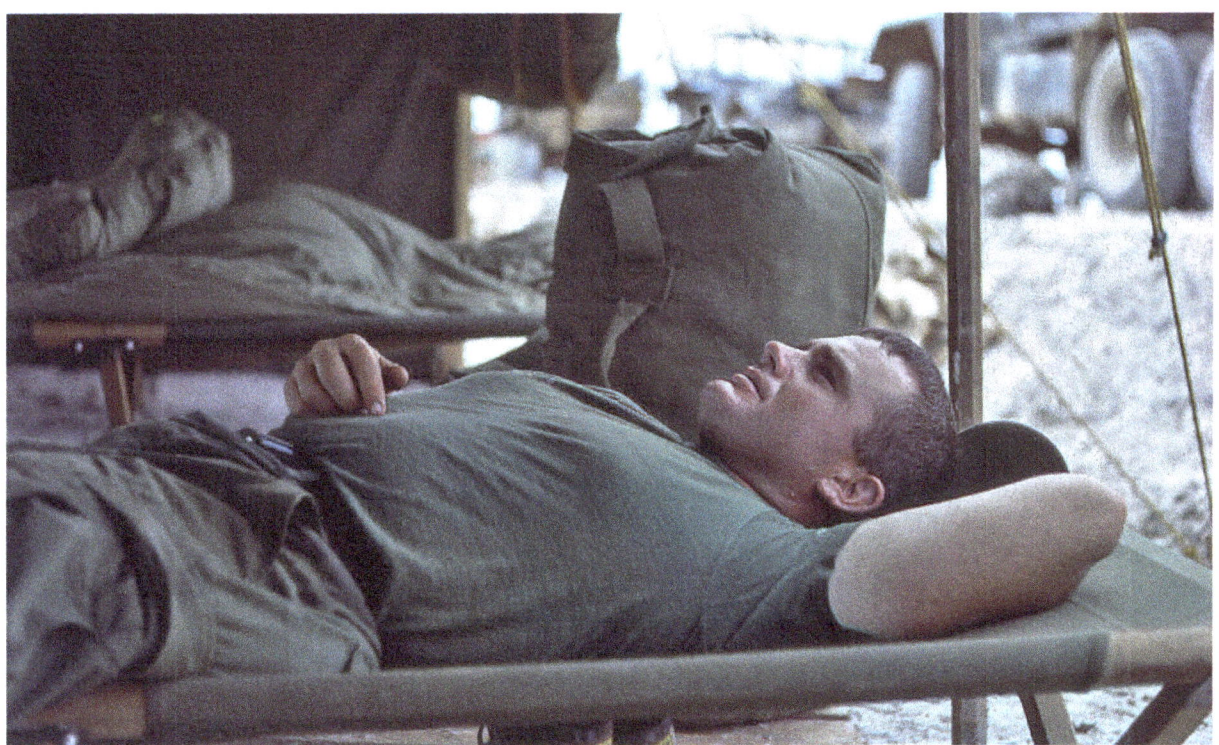
Howden tries to beat the heat

Filling sand bags at Quang Tri

On one exceptionally hot afternoon, the heat was so bad the road was empty. I saw a black speck coming my way through the heat waves. I was lying on my cot, staring at the road disappearing into the haze as it bounced down the highway. Eventually, a man in black pajamas appeared with a sixteen-foot-long tree trunk on his shoulder that must have weighed more than he did. He would bounce it like they do with the yokes that balance on their shoulders with trays or hooks on the ends carrying something. They hopped along so the ends of the yoke, or tree trunk, was on the up bounce when the next step was taken. An ingenious method of moving stuff around without a vehicle. There were few cars or trucks down there, and traffic on Highway 1 had slowed to a trickle. I watched the man and his burden for five minutes before he disappeared into the sweltering heat without stopping for a break. It made me wonder how we could possibly win this war.

Self propelled .105-mm gun at Quang Tri

    Lieutenant McCarthy attended a conference about defending Quang Tri with the Marines and the ARVN. While there, he met an incredibly beautiful doctor who ran an orphanage. Out of the goodness of his heart, or the vastness of his desire, the lieutenant promised to supply the children with excess goods from our unit.

    We did receive mortar and rocket attacks inflicting some damage to our neighbors, but overall, Quang Tri was relatively peaceful. We were preparing to move again when a typhoon hit us, delaying our departure. We closed the tents and hunkered down for the storm. The guns had been busy with missions to the northwest and a few close to the coast. The thunder during the typhoon and the howling wind created a symphony with our 175s.

Soldier By Chance

CAM LO – CAMP CARROLL

On the road to Cam Lo

Once the tents were dry, we packed up and moved north, turning west on Highway 9 near the Song Mieu Giang River. Aside from some beautiful sunsets, our world of color in Quang Tri consisted of olive green and white sand. The glaring sun took the vividness out of the blue sky adding a dullness to it. The emerald green countryside and aqua blue of the river was soothing to the eyes as we followed it most of the way to Cam Lo, cutting south for a few miles to Camp Carroll.

It was easy to see why Vietnam was called the rice bowl of Indochina. The paddies were more extensive here, but nothing compared to the vast fields in the Mekong Delta. This lush land stood in stark contrast to Camp Carroll, a bare patch of rutted, dusty dirt. It had been muddy and would be again at any time. Jimmy Hobbs named it the "Mud Hole."

Soldier By Chance

Fire Base Camp Carroll near Cam Lo

The guns took their place on the edge of this crowded base positioned to fire to the southwest. We set up behind the 175s, unfurling the tent, raising the antenna, and getting ready for work. Sofian wouldn't have to deal with the generator. Camp Carroll had its own power supply.

My crew's sleeping quarters shared a big bunker with a Marine 8-inch FDC section. The 8-inch howitzer shared the same chassis as the 175; the barrels were interchangeable. It shot a shorter, fatter, and heavier projectile. Our gun was designed for distance, whereas the 8-inch was a howitzer whose purpose was to lob its two-hundred pound projo up and over.

Our bunker mates were a wild bunch. I don't know if they found or built the special closet just big enough for a man to stand up in. When our section joined theirs, it was obvious these guys smoked weed down in the bunker instead of in the shitter. They took turns in the closet, while smoke blown in through straws created a chamber of stone-ness. This whole group smoked so much weed, the bunker became such a chamber to the dismay of some of my mates who disapproved of it. The marijuana grown in this country was also incredibly strong. This may or may not have made the rat-infested hole more palatable. They crawled over you in your cot, and once in a while the crack of a 45 jolted you awake blowing one to bits. On one night, a slight scream made me open my eyes to see Murphy with one of these large rodents perched on his head chewing on something. His eyes were wide open with the anticipation that someone would try to shoot this one in the dim light. He finally was released from his frozen state as the rat scurried to someone else's cot.

We were there to support the Marines in the North at Con Tien, in the West at the Rock Pile and the Eastern flanks of Khe Sanh. The Rock Pile was originally a French base with commanding views of the whole area. It was a jagged 1,000-foot-high, solid rock, twin-peaked promontory that dominated the horizon between Khe Sanh and Camp Carroll. The Vietnamese named it "The Wings of Angels," the most significant landmark in I-Corps.

There were 8-inch batteries and some older self-propelled 155s at Camp Carroll. With all our guns and the incoming, this was a very loud base. We were once again within range of the artillery on the other side of the DMZ and it came in sporadically all day.

A GOOD DEED GONE BAD

Vietnamese children orphaned by war in Quang Tri

Lieutenant McCarthy had been busy fulfilling his promise to the doctor in Quang Tri. He was friends with everyone, especially Hulger, the Mess Sergeant who had wheeled and dealed to load a 5-ton with supplies for the orphanage. Hulger drove the truck with four volunteers to help unload. Most of us just wanted to get off the base. Benches folded down in back for passengers. Lieutenant McCarthy rode up front while we sat in back with the supplies.

I remember this as was one of the nicer days; no rain, not too hot, and a sweet smell of wildflowers permeated the air. Vietnam didn't often smell this good. Sergeant Hulger followed the river and eventually turned south on Highway 1. After crossing three bridges, we exchanged the sweet-smelling valley for an endless white sand desert. We turned again heading into Quang Tri, the colonial city built by the French with the orphanage in the center.

As we rode through the town, it was obvious a battle had taken place. Before I arrived in Vietnam, 1500 NVA had attacked and occupied Quang Tri in April of 1967. At the beginning of the Tet Offensive, the 31st of January, 1968, the NVA swarmed into the city again and held it into February, when it was liberated by the 1st Cavalry and the 101st Airborne. I found out years later, that in March of 1972, four NVA Divisions had crossed the DMZ. They moved their artillery within range and Quang Tri was under siege. US air power, including B-52s, protected the city until weather closed in, allowing the NVA to occupy the town again. Massive B52 strikes allowed the ARVN to retake the city in September of 1972. The ARVN suffered over 5000 casualties and in the process, Quang Tri was reduced to a pile of rubble. Today, it has a giant concrete memorial commemorating the thousands of Vietnamese who died there.

Our crew helped the children unload the cargo of condensed milk and everything else the Mess Sergeant could get his hands on. There was a large supply of canned hot dogs and sauerkraut. I met the doctor who motivated McCarthy to set this mission in motion and understood why. She was gorgeous. Our good lieutenant had a sparkle in his eye all day.

On the return trip to Camp Carroll, the conversation about the day sputtered to an end as we drove along the river. Some of us were asleep as I stretched my legs, full of contentment. The appreciation we received from the kids at the orphanage made me feel good for a change about our deeds in this country.

Pesterman, a new man, was sitting across from me. He loaded his weapon and watched the farmers working in the paddies. He then raised his M-16, took careful aim, and shot a bent over woman planting rice. She dropped into the flooded field and didn't move. We sat in horror as a few more were added to his tally. Pesterman removed the empty clip and clapped in a fresh one, smiling as we continued along the river. He leaned back and lit a Marlboro, smoking it like he had just had sex. None of us said anything. One of those moments when you realize the stalwart man you thought you were, didn't exist. My lack of response still bothers me.

Soldier By Chance

I was becoming accustomed to the way we treated the people there. Unless they were shooting at you, we had no way of telling who was on which side. This contributed to the shitty treatment most of them received from most of us. Pesterman's action was a little over the top, to say the least, but when everyone is armed with a lethal weapon, including the assholes, shit happens, and it happened a lot. Hell! We even shot or "fragged" each other! The process of who joined the military wasn't as selective as it is today. That night in our work tent, I spoke to Lieutenant McCarthy about the incident. He had heard the shots and knew what had happened. His advice, "Let it go."

The complications arising from this would not be good. McCarthy may have said something because Pesterman wasn't with us long. He bragged about how successful his political career was going to be in Chicago. I take comfort from the fact that his name isn't familiar.

The hot muggy days at Cam Lo continued when we were told to get ready to move out again. This was another easy transition. The tents had to be struck, and the ammo carriers loaded, as well as the trucks with the supplies and all of our men. After the four guns were set in travel mode with their barrels retracted, we just waited for the order to move out. We were happy to vacate the sleeping bunker we shared with the Marines. I think we all had bugs.

The convoy followed the river when we passed the place where the farmers were murdered. After visiting the orphans, I wondered whether Pesterman didn't think there were enough of them in this country.

Back on Highway 1, we retraced our steps to Dong Ha. The battery was getting proficient at their duties, so it wasn't long before the fire missions resumed as well as work on our bunker.

HOW DID I GET HERE?

A stack of mail was waiting for me at our base in Dong Ha. Apparently, I was still the only member of the College of Marin Drama Department in the military. James Dunn, the director and glue of the theater, had fought and been a Marine Drill Sergeant during the Korean War. He had run rehearsals for the play *Stalag 17* in his uniform and carried a swagger stick. I was one of the POWs the German guards bossed around in this World War II play. The very intense director conducted rehearsals in complete military fashion with formations and discipline for any infraction. We even spent a weekend in the woods marching around while the German guards mistreated us. Method acting to the max. At the time, I thought it was the closest I would ever get to the military.

I tried faint-heartedly to avoid the service. Of course, I didn't want to slosh through the rice paddies getting shot at. Little was known to me about the war raging across the Pacific. My father taught navigation at night to Air Force Officers at Mather Field near Sacramento until I was six. The military was in the background of my life from day one. It was a bigger part of me than any opposition to a war I didn't understand. A sense of duty seemed so honorable.

My father had left my induction orders to join the Army on my doorstep. In spite of the lyrics to the music I loved and my friends trying to persuade me not to go, I went. After selling my 55 Chevy and finding a home for Ralph, my dog, Dad dropped me off at the Oakland Army Depot. He wasn't happy about his delivery.

I left home when I graduated from high school, then after two years of Junior College, got a job as an artist for a printing company in San Francisco. I still worked in Dad's hardware store on weekends. After leaving college, I wasn't crafty enough to avoid a war he already questioned. My dad was much smarter than I was or ever would be. I wish I knew it then. I had no idea that our involvement in this war wasn't such a good idea, let alone a terrible one. My friends just didn't want me to die. As the year eclipsed, I began to realize that no one should be dying in this war.

From that first day in Oakland, a common phrase followed me until I was out of uniform: FTA - Fuck the Army. You heard it all the time. I figured two years of FTA couldn't be healthy, so I made the decision to try my best to be a good soldier, volunteering for everything and earning a stripe right out of basic.

Soldier By Chance

Basic training began with two days of testing that determines your future in the Army. I must have guessed the right answers. I got into a class that resulted in a high MOS and a visit every month with a couple of others to the base commander. We stood at attention as he delivered a pitch to go to OCS, Officer Candidate School. I declined the first two times but during the class in Aberdeen, decided to go for it. After studying every weapon in the giant warehouse, I moved to the OCS barracks and failed my physical. My left eye wasn't so good, and when glasses couldn't correct it, they moved me to another quarters to wait for an assignment.

Three of my classmates were flying to Fort Sill the next day for their future job and my name was also on their orders. We were going to be instructors. Earlier I had pissed them off because of volunteering to go to Vietnam and they were afraid of being sucked along with me. But now . . . Instructor. Wait a minute, why the hell should we be instructors? We had plenty of them starting in Basic. They each wore a blue helmet with a white stripe around it. No KP or guard duty, and fast promotions. Tom Manuel, Ray Brown, and Ernie Decker flew to Oklahoma the following morning excited about their new jobs. I filled out some paperwork and followed them to Dallas and then to Lawton, Oklahoma, on an incredibly bumpy prop airliner. Turbulence would never bother me again. After the bus dropped me off in the middle of Fort Sill, the processing of Private White began. Five months of training had led to this day filled with uncertainty. It took all day to sign in and wait around for a ride to my next assignment. Instructor…this might not be so bad, depending on what I was instructing. It was dark and rain was gently falling when the driver broke the spell.

"So, you're going out to Vietnam Hill?"

"What!"

"Yeah, I'm taking you out there to join a battalion training to go over there."

"Hold on. I'm going to be an instructor, somewhere, instructing . . . something."

"Let me see your orders, 'Mr. Instructor.'"

There are a lot of abbreviations on orders and they can be hard to read.

Apparently!

The driver's reading my orders with a flashlight when he starts laughing. I mean really laughing.

"You dumb shit. Instructor, my ass. You're going to be instructed to go to Vietnam."

"Oh."

Back to square one.

He dropped me off in the rain with the June bugs and First Sergeant Desmond informed me of my new duty. My three classmates were assigned to the other Batteries in the 8th and the 4th to be turret mechanics. I guess they were pissed at me again.

First Sergeant Desmond,
heart and soul of Charlie Battery

CHARLIE - 1

Dong Ha Bridge over Song Mieu Giang River

Word was we would be moving north. Six of us volunteered to go as an advance unit to Charlie-1 (C-1), a firebase on the edge of a refugee village halfway to the DMZ. Mess Sgt. Hulger and some guys on KP who were eager to get out of the "kitchen" rounded out our convoy. The rest of the battery would join us in a week.

There's an old saying in the military, never volunteer for anything. Frankly, I have no idea why this advice eluded me. After only a few days into basic training my hand went up and I'm off to fireman's school to learn how to start and stoke the coal furnaces heating all the barracks in the company. It was cold at Fort Lewis Washington in December. On a twenty-four-hour shift, the big furnaces had to be fed with shovelfuls of coal every two hours. This duty came around every ten days or so.

A week later, my hand popped up again sending me to demolition class for two days, teaching me how to blow things up with everything you can blow it up with. I got a demolition license and rejoined basic training.

Fireman duty exempted me from KP and guard duty and I got to listen to the Drill Sergeants yelling at the rest of the men marching around in the snow from the OR. I would continue to volunteer for everything with no regrets.

Our small convoy led by Lieutenant Carpenter's jeep turned onto Highway 1, which ran through both North and South Vietnam. The very picturesque town of Dong Ha hung over the Song Mieu Gang River and wrapped around to the long bridge crossing it. The large Marine Firebase there had an airfield and medical facilities. The road went due north through flatland and rice paddies to the DMZ, where it abruptly ended. Gio Linh, a Marine base, was there, along with the other Alpha Bases spread out along the border.

C-1 was between Dong Ha and the DMZ, next to a village along the highway that held about five hundred people who had fled North Vietnam. It was a well-kept shantytown made up of discarded military waste, old plywood, shipping crates, and driftwood. Rusty tin roofs and tarps were held in place with sandbags. Frankly, I didn't know how they had acquired all the material to build that place. An explanation would unfold in time as I witnessed the industrious inequity of these people.

The town started at the gates of the base and stretched a quarter mile up the road. Once inside our perimeter, we passed through an ARVN infantry company's compound to our home for the coming months. The ARVN were the South Vietnamese soldiers, Army of the Republic of Vietnam. On the other side of us a Marine Infantry Company had their dug-in quarters. They guarded our perimeter up to the ARVN compound who stood watch over their area. Both the Marines and the South Vietnamese sent out patrols day and night in this remote part of the country referred to as "Leatherneck Square."

The monsoons had yet to end and C-1 was a mud hole, having just been excavated by the Navy engineers. Dozers dug pits for the bunkers and shallow ones the 175s would sit in. For the most part, the bunkers were finished. Rubber membranes covered them and they were backfilled with dirt on the sides and eight feet on top. Layers of sandbags would finish the job, lots of them. The only tent was over the mess area, the one place we congregated.

The big guns in North Vietnam could even be farther back to reach us. These Russian-built cannons were too big to pack down the Ho Chi Minh Trail. Their purpose was to hide out under cover across the border to pound the combined forces of I-Corps along the DMZ.

Carpenter gave us instructions, while the mess detail unloaded cases of C-rations for our stay. The lieutenant's jeep with Kibisky at the wheel headed back to Dong Ha, followed by the cooks in their truck.

We ran communication lines from the guns to our command bunker and headquarters and also helped the Seabees finish the compound. The six of us spent a week getting ready for the rest of the battery. Of course, we would continue to cover everything with sandbags up to the day we moved out of C-1. Our sleeping quarters were deep, about eight steep steps to the bottom. There were plywood bunks three high to sleep fifteen. The ARVN bunkers next to us were the same size, but they managed to squeeze in twice as many. The doorway was open on the south side because the incoming from the north came screaming in with such velocity, the main blast focused on its direction of fire. This was enough protection, unless the enemy projectile was set for 'fuse delay,' in which case fifteen feet of dirt would not have sufficed. At least half of them were set for fuse delay.

The six of us who raised our hands to precede the battery stayed in one bunker at night. It was dark, cold, and damp. Not the kind of weather I expected in Vietnam. We crowded around the only light, a small Coleman lantern. The illumination flares that the Marines and ARVN sent up with mortars were mostly drowned out by the misty rainy nights.

This part of Vietnam was nearly desolate. There wasn't much between Dong Ha and Gio Linh on the DMZ. A few rice paddies and the occasional house. The shantytown next to C-1 wasn't even on our maps. Gio Linh was the only village indicated on them and it was mostly empty with a Marine Fire Base there. This was one of the Alpha Bases, A-2, nicknamed "The Alamo." The constant rains turned a lot of the flat land into a sea of mud, contributing to the bleakness. The closest light was over six miles away in Dong Ha where the electricity ended. The darkness with no starlight between the illumination rounds was beyond imagining. It was impossible to move from one bunker to another without a flashlight. I stepped out one night to take a leak and strayed too far. The black void was so thick it took fifteen minutes to feel my way back through the muck.

Two weeks earlier, we had turned in our very crusty sleeping bags to be cleaned. Their return would be just in time for the warm-up months later. We were sleeping with our boots and uniforms on, but even with a wool blanket, our teeth were chattering. I was offered money for my wool overcoat liner that Supply Sergeant Ozerbeck had given me, but since there wasn't anything to buy up there, I was holding onto it.

The Marines guarded our perimeter, which was substantial, with layers of concertina along with an extensive minefield, and machine gun nests.

One night after a cold meal of ham and motherfuckers, or lima beans, we heard a knock at the top of the stairs. "May I come in?" The request was in perfect English. If he was a bad guy, why bother asking? So we ushered him down. A Vietnamese Warrant Officer introduced himself and told us he was from the ARVN Company next door. This man loved America and knew a lot about it. He was going there after the war to live with relatives in L.A. We welcomed him and noticed him eyeing an object in the room with particular interest—my guitar case.

Just before our excursion to C-1, Lieutenant McCarthy sold me his guitar for two hundred bucks. He wanted more action and was joining a twin forty battery as its CO. The twin 40 was a smaller track vehicle with two 40-millimeter guns mounted on a turret, one of the weapons I studied at Aberdeen. We heard a rumor that his gun had taken a direct hit, thus ending the jovial life of Lieutenant McCarthy.

Our visitor saw the solid case that protected the Martin as it bounced around this country. After a request, he tuned it up. This man could play the guitar. He also knew every song Elvis had recorded, along with Pat Boone. Boy, he loved Pat Boone and the Everly Brothers. Truthfully, he sounded better than all of them, with one of the purest voices I had ever heard. He spoke English with a heavy accent but sang without a trace of it. We were all thrilled with his performance, especially the other volunteers in this advance detail. My beginning attempts to play the guitar must have become tiresome.

As he ascended the stairs to leave, he told us he would be conducting Vietnamese language lessons once a week. After barely passing Spanish in high school, I couldn't imagine speaking Vietnamese. There was still a lot of work to do and the battery would arrive in a few days, so I stashed the invitation in the back of my mind.

We finished the communication lines and worked with the Seabees on the bunkers, including the one we were staying in. The generators arriving with the rest of Charlie Battery would charge the batteries for the radios. Our main source of light would come from Coleman lanterns and the occasional illumination rounds falling to earth outside the wire.

The hard work continued during the day, but once the cloak of nightfall descended, we were in the bunker. Some of us warmed our hands on the Sterno tabs after they heated our C-rations. After a smoke and some bullshitting, it was time to sleep. Willy Darnby and I stayed up later than the other four. We sat around the hissing lantern wrapped in our blankets, exchanging some of the stories of our lives. Willy was a tall lanky man on Sgt. Davis's gun and was one of the oldest in the battery. He had four kids and fell on hard times in Louisiana, got caught in a robbery, and was sent to prison. Another man facing the choice of the Army or jail was Willy, who was thirty-four. His tales of being shot at, chased by dogs, his time in prison, and trying to provide for a hungry family, were in stark contrast to my own stories of epic surf sessions in Santa Cruz and sailing on the San Francisco Bay.

Getting to know a collection of Americans I was unlikely to meet in civilian life was one of the benefits of the war. Willy's age and his size kept him at bay from the guys on his gun who didn't like black men. They didn't like boys from California either, but after six months of active duty, nobody gave a shit where I was from, and I sensed that the racism was waning as well.

The rain never stopped and after a week the Seabees packed up and left. They let us know C-Battery would arrive by noon. This was good news. Back in Dong Ha, Ben Kazazowitz took our laundry into town every week. Our advance detail left before I could exchange my muddy clothes for the laundry bag full of clean and dry uniforms. Kornowski was probably sitting on it, riding up there in the APC.

BATTERY MOVES IN

Charlie Battery in its entirety was moving to C-1, including the Non-Commissioned Officers and the brass, whose presence made the vanguard unit appreciative of our time without supervision. Their arrival, with all the truck and track traffic getting into position, broadened the patch of mud and made it deeper.

Motor pool was busy transporting our supplies, along with powder and ammunition to feed the appetite of the 175s. We emptied the APC of the radios and other equipment to use in our new bunker, including the maps and tables. Fire Direction was now underground to conduct constant fire missions including H & I's at night. We woke up the gun crews with a call on the landline. It could be every ten minutes, or in two hours. They would leave their bunks, slosh through the mud to the gun, get the numbers from FDC, lock and load, and then Ka-boom! Sometimes two but most of the time all four guns would let go. The tube was lowered, breach swabbed, and it was back to bed. These boys, who were all men by this time, became quite efficient at this routine. Some of the crews could carry out the whole operation with three cannoneers.

We were up there to support the Alpha Bases along the DMZ. This became routine for more than a week. One night after chow, I was in our bunker hanging out with the off-duty FDC crew. I was on my upper bunk in the back corner reading *Macbeth* when some Marines from next door came down the ladder looking for me.

"Is there a guy named White down here?"

"Yo, I'm here. What's up?"

"We've been taking Vietnamese classes with the ARVN Warrant Officer. He wanted us to bring you along with your guitar."

"I'm coming."

I persuaded Garfield and Hobbs to join us. They grumbled as they picked up their flak jackets, ammo belts, helmets, and M-16s. We didn't stray too far from the bunkers without this gear. With flashlights, the Marines led us to the ARVN bunker as we sloshed through the mud for more than a hundred yards under our ponchos. We climbed down to their smoky under ground quarters. I don't think they had a mess area, or it was too muddy outside. They cooked their meals on little kerosene stoves in the bunker. I felt crowded in ours, but throw in a few more men cooking strange foods and smoking funky tobacco, well, the stench was indescribable. Somehow they made room for us and we sat down for the class. The ARVN officer was happy to see me, especially when he saw my guitar case. We didn't learn a single word of Vietnamese, but were delighted when he played the Martin and sang for an hour.

Entertainment was hard to come by up there and Hobbs and Garfield thanked me for coaxing them along. The next week the class was cancelled because the soft-spoken officer was killed while on patrol.

Sporadic mortar attacks and a few ground assaults had us still sleeping with our boots on. Infrequent incoming kept us on our toes, but thus far, they hadn't zeroed in on us. Now that our guns had arrived, that situation would change.

We could hear the Marines and the ARVN responding to ground attacks every few nights with small arms fire. The minefield's effectiveness assured us that North Vietnamese soldiers were dying out there. Usually, they could retrieve their dead in the darkness between the illumination rounds the Marines were sending up.

One morning, three bodies wearing suicide packs remained in the minefield below us. I had some knowledge about these satchel charges from the demolition class I had taken in Basic and went along with a few Marines to retrieve the bodies. We followed a map of the minefield and walked light-footed to the deceased attackers.

We stood looking down on the first body. They were enemy Sappers carrying packs loaded with high explosives strapped to their chests. Their objective was to dive into a bunker, or get as close to one of our big guns as possible, and pull the ripcord.

That demolition class also taught me how to blow stuff up and make devices that would do just that. Maybe I could figure this out. A phrase came to mind that would reappear at times like this. "You dumb shit. What are you doing?"

The young sapper's lower half was held together by his uniform, or what was left of it. His left hand firmly gripped a cylinder with a red plunger on the end of it. An exposed wire on the other end led to the C-4. Some of their packs were activated when acid detonated Willy Peter, or white phosphorous. Some badass shit you don't want to get close to. The cylinder on this one generated a spark to the blasting cap, setting off the C-4.

I cautiously pried the device from his stiff, cold hand and rolled the body over, exposing the canvas pack strapped to his chest. The Marines were peering over my shoulder when I suggested they might want to back up. They disappeared in a flash. I opened the satchel and hoped I wasn't in over my head.

It looked simple enough. I gently pulled the blasting cap out of the C-4 and removed the wires from the cap. I cut the pack off the body and handed it to the Marines who had run up after my very loud sigh of relief.

One of them started stabbing the mangled corpse with his bayonet. The dead soldiers were not VC, but NVA, and wore that uniform. After poking the body repeatedly, the soldier rummaged through the uniform and found personal items, including a picture of the dead man's wife and daughter. He distributed the man's money to our small detail. We maneuvered through the minefield to the other young men willing to sacrifice their lives for a cause we didn't understand.

One of them had blown himself up. After removing the remaining satchel, we left their bodies in the mud to rot. The rain intensified, and I was relieved to head back to my bunker.

I was also saddened by the deaths of our young adversaries. By simply being there, we were willing to die in the line of duty. But to strap a bomb on your chest, run through a minefield strafed with machine-gun fire and blow yourself up, was beyond my understanding. I walked back to Charlie Battery in a height of confusion about our involvement in the war.

Before I reached my bunker I realized that, like it or not, we *were* involved, and this overshadowed my sadness. What the fuck, the sappers were headed for Charlie Battery and would have blown us up. The roller coaster of the day's emotions was overshadowed by the exhilaration of being alive.

But let the frame of things disjoint,
Both the worlds suffer,
Ere we will eat our meal in fear,
And sleep in the affliction of these terrible dreams
That shake us nightly; better be with the dead,
Whom we, to gain our peace, have sent to peace,
Than on the torture of the mind to lie
In restless ecstasy.

William Shakespeare, *Macbeth*

CON TIEN

Highway 1 - North to the DMZ

A week later, I had just climbed into my bunk after a twelve-hour shift when Leighton from Sergeant Horner's gun called out from the top of the stairs. Leighton was one of the boys I had avoided in the early days at Fort Sill.

"Hey, Flower Man, do you want to be my guard on a trip up north?"

It didn't take long to gather everything I had just stashed at the foot of my bunk to regroup and join Leighton outside the bunker.

During breakfast, he told me about our detail. We were taking some Marines from next door up to one of the Alpha Bases, Con Tien. The compound was under intense artillery bombardment, and after delivering the ten infantrymen, we would return with five of their dead brothers.

"Are we going up there by ourselves?" I asked.

"Don't worry, man. We have ten Marines with us and the 50 is a badass weapon!"

"Ah . . . Hey, Leighton, are we bringing anyone back with us who's breathing?"

My driver scratched his head and thought for a moment.

"Well, Horner woke me up after Lieutenant McCreedy ordered the detail. I don't ask questions, man."

I had a few. But I knew that when someone doesn't ask questions, it's unlikely he has answers. Especially Leighton.

We met the grunts patiently waiting by the ammunition carrier. Each 175 had one, designed to carry a very heavy load. It was a diesel track vehicle with a flat front and a bench seat for the driver and a few others. A canvas top covered the whole thing. The 50-caliber machine gun was right behind the seat on top. It rotated on a turret, the first turret I had studied in that giant building in Aberdeen.

I uncovered the gun, loaded the long belt of ammo and gripped the handles to steady myself as we drove out the gate past the refugee town towards the top of South Vietnam. Although it was clear and hot, the road was a muddy mess. Half the time it was raining.

Big white clouds separated, allowing the sun to shine through patches of blue. They suddenly converged into a dark mass and spit heavy rain, only to disperse and wait for the process to begin again.

We motored up this desolate road through flat wetlands past Gio Linh to the border of the DMZ. Marines were gathering for the journey to Con Tien. The sky turned gray and it rained while we waited. The M-548 was not a combat vehicle but was designed to carry the heavy ordnance for the 175s and 8-inch howitzers. The riflemen in the back assumed defensive positions and two stood up top with me. One of them told me he felt vulnerable in this vehicle and didn't like it. It occurred to me that I might want to think about some of these details before I jumped into them. Maybe next time.

I couldn't get small enough realizing what a perfect target I was sitting up there. All of a sudden, my flak jacket felt useless. As the diesel idled, I watched a Marine crossing the road when he went into a hole and sank down to his waist in mud. After a 5-ton was backed up, it took two men to pull him out.

Along the muddy road to Con Tien

As we neared this junction, there were more and more of the craters created by the 1000-pound bombs dropped from the B52s. These missions were called Arclight and at our first camp at Dong Ha, they were obliterating the DMZ. We saw the vapor trails from the giant bombers eight miles up on their way north. If they weren't visible, we could hear and feel the 1000-pounders carpet bombing this area. Huge plumes of black smoke starting from right to left blasting the contents of what would become a deep crater skyward. Some of these divots were filled with twenty feet of water.

When there were enough of us to continue, we plowed through the muddy trough with three five-tons loaded with material to build more bunkers. The mud was so deep the space between the tracks was scraped glassy flat by the bottoms of this small convoy. Part of the road was dug out below ground level to allow cover for traffic like us. The two Marines stepped down and joined the soldiers below. I felt like one of those metal ducks you try to hit with a BB gun at the county fair sitting up top with the 50. The vehicles were out of sight, but there I was, bobbing along the DMZ. I'm guessing it could have been ten miles from the junction to Con Tien. We came across an occasional small tree that hadn't been flattened between the craters. The rain stopped and within minutes it was clear and hot again.

The faint thunder of artillery bombardment could be heard over the roar of the engine pushing us through the mud. As we got closer, the constant shelling of the Marine firebase began to drown out the engine and the clattering tracks. The explosions were relentless—two or more every minute—with an occasional lull.

The ammo carrier crested a rise called the "Hill of Angels." The view was unobstructed to the coast in the East, the Annamite Mountains in the West, and the DMZ in the North. This base was vulnerable because the NVA cannons in North Vietnam had greater range than our artillery and was safe from counter battery fire. Before I arrived in-country, Con Tien had been heavily attacked on the 8th of May, 1967, the anniversary of the fall of the French fort at Dien Bien Phu in 1954. Two battalions of NVA with flame throwers cut through the wire and hand-to-hand combat took place. The Marines held the position at great costs to both sides. After the war, the Vietnamese government built the Trung Son cemetery on the site, containing 10,000 graves of NVA soldiers.

We looked down on what was called "Death Valley" in Con Tien. This wasn't a small base; I'd have to guess a battalion with infantry, mortars, 105s, and tanks with the 9th Marines.

There were many bunkers like ours spread out randomly with rubber membranes hanging over them. Dirt was pushed around the sides and dumped on top, with sandbags hurriedly thrown over everything. At C-1, some of our officers went to great pains to make sure the bags covering ours were lined up perfectly. They could give a shit here. There were a few soldiers sloshing through the mud, but if these guys didn't have to be out, they were hunkered down underground.

We idled for a moment, gazing at the Marine encampment. C-1 was a muddy mess but nothing like this place. An explosion would blast a ton of orange mud in all directions. Count to twenty and another shower of mud and shrapnel was redistributing another piece of Vietnam. If you were unlucky enough to be stationed here, you soon realized that death could come a knockin' at any time.

Marine Fire Base - Con Tien

Marines reporting-in to Con Tien

The Russians supplied the North Vietnamese Army with three different artillery pieces capable of reaching Dong Ha and C-1, let alone Con Tien. They also had separate powder charges like the 175, but they did have multiple projectile types. It was hard to tell how many of them were relentlessly shelling Con Tien. The one hundred pounders made their way into the Alpha base all day long. These guns were even farther away, easier to hide, and changing positions at night made it harder for us to keep track of them.

We were guided to a bunker in the center of the base and helped load the five body bags into the back as the soldiers we delivered reported in. Two of the Marines were killed at a battle zone inside the DMZ called the 'Marketplace.' The other three died at Con Tien. Some of our first fire missions after we arrived at Dong Ha back in August had leveled the area around the Marketplace. The Marines were engaged in a major battle up there, but it didn't compare to the one that raged in March of 1967 before I arrived in Vietnam. Our B-52s pulverized the area killing thousands of NVA soldiers. A lot of Marines died up there. For that matter, Con Tien was equally as dangerous.

Soldier By Chance

We were accustomed to "incoming." Nothing like this, but enough so we didn't embarrass ourselves when some came in close enough to shower us with mud.

Loaded with our sad cargo, we watched the bright orange flashes blasting mud everywhere, accompanied by the whoosh, the concussion, and the hissing of the shrapnel landing here and there as the NVA readjusted slightly while reloading.

We departed Con Tien by ourselves, which seemed strange after the big deal that was made about convoying in. I was very alert gripping the handles on the 50, my personal favorite, but I was hoping not to use it on this trip. The men in the back were not at the ready for our return to C-1.

The ammo carrier we were riding in was really noisy with the diesel engine under the seat and the tracks themselves made a hell of a clatter. It was too loud to talk to Leighton about the boys in the body bags, allowing me reflect on the day as I sat up on top. So far, our battalion had lost a few men, and we had five dead Marines in the back who were all killed the day before. They could very well be zipping up another bag before our return to base. Leighton turned the ammo carrier south when we reached the highway. I would not venture this far north again, but Charlie Battery would be stationed at Con Tien later. The Marines left Vietnam in 1969 and the Army took over their positions. When the U.S. began de-escalating, the 8th and the 4th handed over their guns to the South Vietnamese who took over the Alpha and Charlie Bases. The battalion returned to Fort Sill and disbanded. It wouldn't be long before the North Vietnamese occupied the firebases and added equipment we left behind to theirs, becoming one of the largest armies in the world. We had spent years shipping war supplies and equipment over there and ended up leaving all of it.

Back inside our gates, we delivered our cargo to the Marine Company next door. That night, I was back at work in FDC.

Leighton came over during a lull and hung out in the bunker anxious to talk about our trip to the DMZ. Lieutenant Briggs, Kornowski, Kellerman and Hobbs listened as we described the Marine Fire Base. We all agreed that our world at C-1 wasn't so bad.

It wouldn't be long before Kellerman would have his own story to tell, and Charlie Battery was about to experience some of the wrath leveled on Con Tien.

INCOMING – THE SIEGE

Our routine would soon change dramatically. One afternoon, a solo artillery round landed one hundred yards in front of our wire. The next day, same time, another landed sixty yards behind us. When a forward observer calls in a fire mission, he adjusts after the first round. Rather than try to hit you dead on, he will overcompensate until you are bracketed. Artillery 101. On the third day, once it was light enough to hide their bright muzzle blast, three guns dug in somewhere on the other side of the DMZ were assigned to pound us. They never missed. Three rounds at a time spread out sporadically during the day. There was no routine, so it was easy to get caught out in the open. Bam! Bam! Bam! Maybe in five minutes, or two hours, but you knew they were coming.

C-1 was in a line from east to west and less than a quarter mile long. The North Vietnamese had the distance or elevation of their gun barrels dialed in. All they had to do was swing their guns from side to side, drop or add a little to cover every square inch of C-1. Our four guns were spread out in the center on the northern side facing the enemy, with the rest of the battery spaced behind. You don't want to be in front of a 175 when she goes off. Our neighbors' bases were more condensed and they suffered heavier casualties than we did. We could hear their vehicles braving the bombardment to transport dead and wounded to Dong Ha along with a few medevacs.

Everyone had a bunker. I slept in one and worked in another. The mess area, six-seat outhouse, and the guns themselves, were the most vulnerable.

Sergeant Davis had a close call when all three enemy rounds landed near his gun. Two of his men were wounded by shrapnel and rushed to Dong Ha in Desmond's jeep and Westmoreland's 5-ton to round out the convoy. The gun was damaged but it could have been a lot worse. Two of the one hundred pounders blew up underground with fuse delay.

Motor Pool and the mechanics were in Dong Ha. Anything that wasn't involved with firing the guns was down there. Aside from the weekly convoy to resupply our ammunition for the relentless consumption of the guns, nothing else went in or out unless it was an emergency.

Nelson, our turret repairman, and Ernie Decker, the turret mechanic from Service Battery, came up to get the 175 back online. Decker was from my class back in Aberdeen. He drove a 3/4-ton with Nelson, supplies, parts, and tools. I joined them to help repair the gun. Without some divine assistance, I wouldn't be helping; this would be my job. We replaced damaged hydraulic lines and some electronics. Our repairs were interrupted when we were forced to dive for cover as a fresh set of three came screaming in. The gun was pockmarked from shrapnel, but we got it to run and fire before dark.

Davis borrowed a man from Bird's gun and was back in action. I was on duty that night, so Decker got to see FDC at work. After a while, he hit the rack on a sheet of plywood in my bunker. He left with the Marines in the morning and drove his truck back to Dong Ha with Nelson. Later, Decker would write me a letter after being transferred to Pleiku, but I lost track of him.

When the ammo was delivered, it was like a circus unloading and getting the hell out of there. They didn't want to be slowed down by towing a water trailer which made no sense to me. Making the run at dawn or dusk when the enemy had shut down their guns, opened up the chance of ground attacks on Highway 1. We were never on the road after dark.

It did not take long to run out of food and water. Even the C-rations started to disappear. The cooks did have a large supply of canned hot dogs. Well, they almost tasted like hot dogs. The only thing worse was the canned sauerkraut.

The combination became breakfast and dinner. Along with running for your life to eat, or to get back to the bunkers, the mess tent was empty during daylight, so scratch lunch.

We ate our dogs and kraut right after sunup and just before dark with a blackout to help conceal us from ground attacks. We hoisted five-gallon jerry cans of water to a guy on a platform, who dumped them into a 55-gallon drum until full. We would pull a stick out of the hole at the bottom to take an occasional shower.

In Dong Ha, the camp had evolved to the point where the gasoline drip heaters used for the dishwater warmed the showers. At C-1 cold showers were the first casualties of the water crisis, along with the dishwater. Holger started serving our meals on paper plates. Cold, of course, without hot water to cook them. Cases of C-rations started arriving with the ammo delivery and we now had a menu. We dry shaved because heaven forbid, you go unshaven. There was just enough of the brown heavily chlorinated water to drink.

If you stood at the top of the stairs going down to the bunkers, the stench was breathtaking. To make matters worse, there were those who didn't visit the shitter during daylight. Small piles of it sat at the bottom of the stairs until dark when the depositors were persuaded to clean it up. A couple of fights broke out over this.

Soldier By Chance

    Tensions were running high. Miraculously, we suffered no fatalities, with just a few wounded. With the enemy's Forward Observer adjusting their fire, Charlie Battery would have been in big trouble. After he established the confines of our perimeter, their Observer must have high-tailed it. They were randomly shooting into our base and we were randomly trying to pinpoint the weapons threatening us. The difference being we had no idea of their whereabouts. A night ground attack seemed imminent, so our M-60s joined the Marines on the perimeter, and the ammo carriers had their 50s protecting the big guns. We were back on rotating guard duty.

The one saving grace about the North Vietnamese artillery was they could not fire at night. Their huge muzzle blast was impossible to hide, even under cover. Our guns were out in the open, so even though the crews had to work with flashlights, they could fire all night long while the artillery across the DMZ had to cool off until morning. It wasn't long before most of us became accustomed to the constant shelling. The guns shooting at us were closer to the border and harder to conceal compared to the pieces firing on Con Tien, so they hid out for a while between barrages. There is no way we could have survived the constant shelling Con Tien was under.

Finally, our supply trucks brought in some water trailers. We wouldn't be taking showers until the siege was broken, but we could drink, cook, and clean our mess kits with the brown-green water.

By now, a lot of the men smoked marijuana. Those who chastised the evil weed earlier were now ready to partake in its influence. This was in part due to the constant shelling and our remote location. No milk, no beer, no girls, and not much else.

I first discovered the pot vendors when we were stringing concertina wire on the perimeter at Dong Ha. A farmer with a water buffalo, not required, would pass by, and for a buck, you had ten joints with seeds encased in a plastic pouch. We were much more isolated up there, so I don't know where all the weed came from, but come dusk, the seeds were popping on the bunker tops.

The only contact with the village next door was when Ben Kazazowitz took laundry there once a week, but Ben and the laundry stayed put during the siege.

The outhouse served two functions—the second was a safe place to smoke grass. *Safe* being a relative term. This was without a doubt the most dangerous place to be during incoming. Much the same as dropping your drawers and sitting out in the open. The thin plywood sides had screens at the top so someone could stand on the bench with the holes and keep a lookout. During a lull, twelve men might be jammed in there. Pity the guy who actually had to take a crap.

One afternoon, I was doing a poor job of standing watch when Staff Sergeant Breem, the NCO in charge of all four guns, *surprised* us. He bashed the door open yelling, "Got ya!" through the smoke. He then smiled and went up the hill to the officers' and NCO's shitter, laughing all the way.

HEART ATTACK!!

The consequences of getting caught smoking weed were severe. There was a special prison in the south for such offenders. The whistle of a fresh barrage brought us back to our senses as we flew out of the crapper booking it to the nearest bunker. I remember diving down the stairs laughing my ass off. I was more rattled by the sergeant's intrusion than the accompanying three surprises from the North.

Jimmy Hobbs and Tom at C-1 Bunker

SANDBAG RUN

Filling sandbags along the river near Dong Ha

We didn't have sand at C-1, but there was an abundance of dirt and mud, and a lot of our off-duty time was spent filling nylon bags with it. During unpredictable incoming, this was too dangerous to do in daylight. At night, we put out as little light as possible. The guns even operated with flashlights covered by red lenses.

After two weeks into the siege, Westmoreland woke me up early one morning. Trying not to disturb anyone else, he stood on the lower bunk and shook me.

Soldier By Chance

"Sandbag run. You game?"

Westmoreland was a mechanic and had been transferred from Sergeant Horner's gun to Motor Pool before we left Oklahoma.

I lay there for a second, having just gone to sleep after my shift.

"Come on, Flower Man. Let's go for a ride."

"Sure. Go tell Sergeant Hulger to warm up some dogs and sauerkraut for us while I let Lieutenant Briggs know."

After splashing some cold water on my face and reporting to Briggs about my whereabouts, it was time for chow. Lieutenant Briggs took over for Lieutenant McCarthy when we moved to C-1. We were lucky to get another officer as fair as the well-liked McCarthy.

I was a guard on the first convoy of two trucks to a riverbed for sandbags at Dong Ha. Our original base had lots of dirt also. Dirt bags work, but there's nothing like a good sandbag.

About thirty or so old men, women, and children would be waiting with a honcho who was done or exempt from the Army. After throwing a couple bundles of bags down, the locals would fill, tie them off, and throw the full bags back on the truck. Their payment was usually two cases of C-rations, one for each truck. The honcho would distribute the goods as we were on the way back to base.

Westmoreland knew I liked this detail and considering the rocky start in Oklahoma where he wanted to smash my face in, we were now friends. After some breakfast, before the daily barrage began, we took his five-ton out the gate. I was uneasy as we departed by ourselves. When I questioned Westmoreland, he told me Lieutenant McCreedy ordered him to leave for the village before the morning incoming, load up, and wait outside the gate for a barrage to end and scoot back in. After chow, a crew would unload and stack the fresh sandbags in the full moonlight. Uh oh, McCreedy again. He had been at odds with me for some time and was going to be the death of me yet.

Okay . . . this didn't feel right. But it shouldn't take long to fill one truck and get the hell out of there, I thought. So much for thinking things through.

Sandbag Run at Dong Ha

There were little open-air restaurants just outside our gates consisting of one or two tables and some rusty chairs covered by a canvas tarp for the South Vietnamese company. We crossed the highway, it's called that, but hours could pass without anything on it this far north. Westmoreland drove us to the outskirts of the town a hundred yards from the hooches. They saw us coming and within minutes it seemed the same thirty from Dong Ha were waiting to go to work, although dressed in warmer clothes. I threw the bundles of bags off the truck and the villagers scurried to fill them. Westmoreland stayed in the driver's seat and opened a paperback, but before long, he was sound asleep.

Around this time, the daily artillery attack had begun. When the first round screamed overhead, I came close to hitting the ground. The villagers got a kick out of this and they all laughed a lot. Every shell destined for our base soared over this village, and most of the outgoing from C-1 also whistled overhead. Before the first barrage of three was over, I had begun laughing with the villagers, breaking the ice. Some spoke English and asked about San Francisco, whether I was married, my sisters. My God, they were curious.

Dong Ha

After handing out most of my Camels to the women and kids, the crowd really lit up. This was the reason I liked sandbag runs, to be with the villagers like this as they worked and communicated, intensely passionate in their laughter, sadness, or anger. A happy and proud people, but fierce when provoked. Especially the women. I found them to be more intense than the men.

Tom White with village kids near C-1

HUANG ON

It wasn't long before we were loaded with sandbags, but there was a problem. I dumped off two bundles and the rest of the pile wouldn't fit on the truck. I woke Westmoreland informing him of our dilemma. He was still a little groggy and looked at me like I knew what the fuck to do. I did know I wasn't going to be the one to tell Lieutenant McCreedy we had left a pile of sandbags in the Ville because I dropped off too many bundles. I was already skating on thin ice with him.

We stood there in front of the mound of bags with thirty people staring at us waiting for our next move and their C-rations. This was not good. If we left, by the time the truck was out of sight, the bags would be gone, and a few more hooches would be surrounded by them.

Westmoreland, we called him General, and I were at a loss. Okay . . . the only solution, the dumbest anyway, was to take the load to the base, get an empty truck, and return for the rest, and for me. I would stay behind to guard the pile. This plan made me feel uncomfortable and I was not reassured when the villagers thought it was a great idea. However, the wrath of McCreedy over some dumb sandbags was scarier than being left alone in the village.

The General drove off leaving me standing next to a mountain of sandbags and thirty refugees from North Vietnam. They were laughing a lot, at what, I'm not sure. Possibly the daisies I'd drawn on my helmet cover to replace the peace sign that had offended Lieutenant Carpenter on the *Upshur*. Another cause for amusement could have been this G.I. left alone in the village.

I talked with one of the honchos for a while. His English was just adequate enough to tell me about some of his five years fighting the VC and the NVA before he was wounded. Apparently, he was wounded a lot. You had to be too old or too young to avoid serving in the ARVN. Or, you had to be wounded . . . a lot. A group of women started screaming at each other about something and the old soldier entered the fray to calm them down.

Firing up one of my remaining Camels and sitting down on some cold sandbags, I noticed a man coming towards us. He walked across the field of white sand and held out both hands as he approached me. I placed my cigarette on my seat and held his small hands as three more rounds made their way into our firebase. All the villagers waiting with me knew him well. From the way they treated him, it was clear they held him in high regard. He spoke perfect English and introduced himself as Huang On. He was attending the University of Hue studying to be a lawyer and was visiting his family for a few days. He had watched the truck drive off and was surprised to see me there alone. He came over to make sure I was all right.

Huang On didn't smoke, leaving me my last Camel. Soon we were deep in conversation. He had moved to Hue years earlier to attend the university before his family came here when the war intensified. Their farm was just above the DMZ, a very volatile area, so it was either move north or south. Most everything was left behind. A few precious family heirlooms and the tools necessary to create a new life were the only things they carried with them. When our jets dropped bombs on their farm, his two sisters were killed along with his mother. That was the day they started moving across the border. They hoped to go back after the war, if there was anything to go back to.

The provincial capital of Hue was apparently a very beautiful ancient city built by the old cultures. Huang On couldn't say enough about it and hoped I could visit. He wanted to know about my family, education, and my life. We laughed a little and then became serious because of the country's predicament. War is serious.

As another barrage whistled overhead, I was reminded of my situation. Westmoreland wouldn't be back for an hour. The NVA gun crews busted butt, and in quick succession, unleashed three more into C-1. They were hard at work.

Then Huang On invited me to come home with him and meet his family. I laughed.

"Out of the question. I have to guard our load here."

He rose, spoke to the villagers, and then assured me that our precious cargo would be safe. The smiling people nodded their heads in agreement and would notify us when the general returned.

I had a back and forth battle in my mind as I smoked my last Camel realizing I was probably safer with my new friend than hanging out in the open.

I watched the people as they waited for Westmoreland's return. The banter between them was nonstop, with occasional outbursts of anger. But the sounds of laughter permeated the calm between the whistling projectiles soaring overhead in each direction. I studied the kind face of Huang On, and we read each other's mind as we stood at the same time and walked towards the village. He talked about the hardships the war had bestowed on his two countries, making it clear he was not from the North or South, but was Vietnamese. A group of children followed us as we made our way across the sandy plain. The kids waited outside as we ducked through the entrance of a house on the edge of the village.

His stepmother was tending a small fire on the floor. Few families were intact here. She jumped up and backed against the wall, but after seeing Huang On relaxed a little. She timidly bowed and after a big smile, went back to tending the fire. Her teeth were shockingly red, like a lot of people in this country who chewed the stimulating and addictive betel nut. A plywood flap held open by a stick was meant to relieve the hooch of smoke, which it didn't. Three men were squatting around another small fire smoking opium in the opposite corner. Two left in a hurry as Huang On's father graciously introduced himself.

I was guided into a larger room with bamboo mats spread out on the floor, one ornately carved double bed, also with bamboo mats and what looked like a restaurant booth against the wall. The mahogany booth had a table with benches surrounded by intricately carved sides and posts with a blue and white silk top. I was offered a seat, Huang On sat next to me and his father sat across from us. My host's little brother stood behind his dad peering over his shoulder at me.

Huang On's stepmom immediately brought in a tray with three glasses and a bottle of Jack Daniels. They assured me the whiskey had been removed and replaced with Vietnamese wine. Papa San filled the small glasses and after all three clinked together, we drank the local wine. Wow! It sure tasted like Jack Daniels to me. Come to think of it, I had never heard of Vietnamese wine. Another barrage soared overhead.

Papa San talked about the war dividing his family and Huang On translated. Some had chosen to stay in the North, but others didn't survive to make the choice. Every day was uncertain, let alone the years to come. He enthusiastically told the story of their journey here just before all hell broke loose. On the final trip south with the last of the possessions they could carry, twenty B-52s pulverized the DMZ right after they made it across. And that was that. Highway 1 was officially closed crossing the demilitarized zone.

Another topic was the scary nights here. NVA or VC patrols could be heard walking through the village in the darkness. Mama San was listening and rushed in to emphatically tell me that one of her friend's husbands was VC and would sneak in after dark to have sex! Huang

On smiled. He had known this man since childhood. It was nice to know that sometimes friendships can prevail in a nation divided by war. And Mama San . . . could speak English! Number One Son had a hiding place to ride out the dicey nights and Papa hinted of an AK at hand. Wind blew smoke from the kitchen fire into the room and it swirled about. Huang On told me the smoke helped keep the bugs out.

Mama San kept bringing treats in for us. I politely ate what I could but had no idea what they were. After describing the ingredients to me . . . I still had no idea. They kept assuring me that the second Westmoreland returned, we would know. He had already been gone for hours. The young son never took his eyes off me as he listened to the conversation, apparently also understanding English. I noticed the M-16 between my legs and remarked to them how for a moment I had forgotten about the war I was in. Huang On laughed and told me how my presence really reminded them of it. All of us had a good laugh over that.

Another three rounds howled overhead and I stood and thanked them. The base was really taking a pounding today. It was time to get back with or without Westmoreland. After shaking hands with the men, including little brother, Huang On's stepmother surprised me when she squeezed my hand and wouldn't let go.

Walking back to the pile of sandbags where the waiting villagers were sitting, ten kids ran up to me screaming wildly. "Come quick! Come quick!"

I could see smoke in the center of the village as they tugged at my uniform. There was no sign of Westmoreland. I was beginning to feel comfortable in this town as I followed them to a small hooch with its palm frond roof ablaze. The Vietnamese are short people. I slung my rifle, found a long board, and began to beat the flames, while the town folk were throwing sand on them without success.

By God, I put the fire out to the applause of thirty people, no less. Invitations came my way from villagers wanting to share their hospitality. I could see the pile of sandbags without a truck to throw them in. One of the young girls that had followed me from Huang On's house tugged on my flak jacket. She pointed to a distinguished old man who was standing nearby and held my hand as she led me over to him. He bowed and I could tell he was humbly inviting me to his home. Those that could speak English assured me they would let me know when Westmorland returned. We walked to the Old Man's house as his grandchildren and the kids circled around us. His daughter knew I was coming and a table was set with three glasses,

Soldier By Chance

steaming hot tea, and more unrecognizable delights. I sat down and we smiled at each other as they made reference to the rounds soaring overhead. Apparently, they also noted the increasing incoming pouring into C-1. We sipped our tea and I politely tasted some of the offerings that were quite good. The old man and his daughter spoke to each other while the kids whispered back and forth. A salvo of .175mm rounds from C-1 whistled overhead. I put on my helmet, thanked them, and picked my way through the children to the door.

Still no sign of Westmoreland. As I walked back to the waiting villagers who were as anxious as I was to go home, it seemed the incoming from the North was ending for the night. It was getting late, time to hurry back to C-1 by myself.

Damn, I wish I hadn't given all my smokes away.

I was saying goodbye to the townsfolk, hoping they would let me go without paying them when Westmoreland came bouncing in at full speed. The pile was quickly loaded and the people were happy that he had brought their cases of C-rations. I was relieved that I didn't have to run back to base. We scurried home in the semi-darkness.

I gave the General a look of gratitude for coming back. He told me that after returning to C-1 with the sandbags, the incoming was so intense, he jumped out of his truck and ran to a bunker. When the last barrage ended, he snuck out of the compound in an empty five-ton to get me. "I had to come back for you. If the Captain found out I left you in the Ville, well, I would 'a been screwed. I guess it wouldn't have been so good for you either, eh?" The look of gratitude didn't seem enough, and I wanted to hug the big guy. He probably would have slugged me.

BAD DAY AT C-1

Tom White and Sergeant Bird (center) with two of his gun crew

This was a bad day for Charlie Battery. I could hear the ordnance hurling over me all day, but had no idea where it was landing. As we booked it back, Westmoreland told me about the day's events. A brand-new boy who had only been a few days in-country was killed, and he hadn't even been assigned a position yet. So far, he was just filling sandbags. Sergeant Bird, one of the 175 chiefs, was medevacked to Dong Ha. He lost or would lose both legs. His 175 was destroyed and two of his crew were seriously wounded. Bird was one of the most liked men in our battery if not *the* most liked. A big jovial dude from Texas with a horse ranch who felt it was his duty to fight in this war. Sergeant Bird volunteered for three years, but his tour was over now. The South Vietnamese guarding the gate gave us the once over before letting us in. This was way too late to be returning to base.

I remembered the new boy who had been killed. Just days earlier during incoming fire, our least popular lieutenant had ordered him to restack sandbags dislodged by the exploding ordnance. Lt. McCreedy had a gift for being an asshole, assigning tasks out of spite that drove you crazy.

Later that night while on duty in FDC, Kibisky summoned me to report to the Captain. We walked to headquarters and met Westmoreland outside. *Oh-Oh. Something to do with today's fiasco in the village.* I was hoping no word about it had made it to the OR. He laid into us for quite a while for being so reckless. Apparently, Lieutenant McCreedy felt some of this wrath for ordering the detail. This was not good. You don't want to piss off guys like McCreedy. He had a legitimate gripe with me, however, for throwing two bundles off the truck.

My experience with Huang On and his family was something I will never forget. All of that aside, if the General and I had half a brain we would have driven away from the pile of sandbags and never mentioned them. I went back to work to hear the recap of the day's events.

The pitch of Jimmy Hobbs' voice went up a notch as he told me how the new guy had died. He was carried into our work bunker where he bled out. The boy couldn't speak but his eyes were wide open, making contact with those around him. His chest was ripped open and you could actually see his lungs. There was no crying out in pain, just the end of a quest for breath and eyes gazing into *the nothing*. I only saw him a few times and didn't know his name, but the bloodstain on the wooden floor would remind me of that day long after the red mud of Vietnam erased most of it.

After my shift ended at 6 AM, I lay in my top bunk under ten feet of dirt and sand absorbing the day's vivid memories. I liked seeing the Vietnamese people as much as possible. The previous day in the village had afforded me this more than I could have ever imagined. Huang On's family spoke very little about the Communists who we were fighting. The farm they left had been in their family for generations and they were waiting for the war to end so they could go back to it. They held no hatred for the other side that I could see. This was another war between the tribes and we were caught in the middle of it. It would end and life would get back to normal one day, seemed to be their attitude.

Before I dozed off, Sergeant Bird and the new boy filled my thoughts. Especially after Garfield told me how he had been killed. For some reason, probably because he was a dick, Lieutenant McCreedy was constantly on the new guy's ass. Some sandbags had been blown off one of the bunkers and the lieutenant ordered him to restack them between barrages when he was caught in the open and killed. Shortly after this incident, McCreedy had an armed guard from another unit trailing him and sleeping at the foot of his bunker.

NAVY DROPS IN

The rain had returned, but only lasted a few days. On a clear late afternoon when it was safe to venture out, the migration to the bunker tops had begun. The setting sun behind the western mountains cast orange and yellow spectrums of light into the navy-blue sky. As seeds popped here and there, we heard fighter jets above us. You could make them out slowly circling overhead with red flashing lights on their wingtips. We didn't give it much thought; an air attack was the last thing we expected. After the third low pass, I noticed dark objects tumbling from the lead aircraft. One landed between us and the ARVN and the other hit them dead on. WHAM! WHAM! On the next pass, the second plane dropped its load closer to the village. Each plane carried two 500-pound bombs.

The explosions were deafening and my ears rang for days. The big pieces of shrapnel flying around froze us in our tracks as they screamed by. Some of them weighed more than five pounds. Charlie Battery was kissed by lady luck. Those 500-hundred pounders could have easily destroyed our three remaining guns and wiped the rest of us off the map.

We assumed they were MIGs, but months later I learned that the Navy had launched the two jets off a carrier in the Gulf of Tonkin.

Bombing us didn't make any sense. The North Vietnamese didn't have bases in the open like ours. This was a major blunder, one of the many that are inevitable during the fog of war. It was amazing that no one was killed because shrapnel was everywhere.

An ARVN bunker was hit, but luckily they had just left for a night patrol. A week earlier, their luck wasn't so good when an NVA projo with fuse delay penetrated one, killing thirty-five.

While we didn't have casualties, the village next door did. The following day, our Motor Pool came up from Dong Ha to transport over fifty wounded to the Marine doctors there. They didn't have to worry about the incoming artillery that only landed inside the wire of C-1. The people in this town dealt with their dead. I never found out how many were accidentally killed. My friends lived on the other side of the village. I hoped they were okay.

SIEGE ENDS

North Vietnamese Artillery firing the D-74, their .122-millimeter gun | North Vietnam Army photo

After the loss of Sergeant Bird and his gun, we limited our daylight fire missions to support the ARVN and Marine patrols. Spotter planes and forward observers were seeking the three guns dialed in on us. We finally succeeded in destroying them, or some of them, or they moved elsewhere.

Kellerman was filling in for a Marine RTO who had been killed in the siege. I heard him get up and leave the bunker around one-thirty in the morning to join the infantry next door for a two-day patrol. When Kellerman wasn't on duty, it was my turn to man the radios.

My FDC crew got up at dawn, dry shaved, and made our way to the bunker to take over Howden's shift. After C-rations we sent some H&I missions to the guns and waited. It was midmorning. I was sitting by the radios reading a Graham Greene novel while Kornowski was writing a letter home. Murphy was half asleep with his head on the map table. Maybe he was completely asleep. Garfield was leaning back in his chair also reading and Lt. Briggs was in the OR with Captain Gerber. The rain had stopped. A few barrages from the North and Murphy's snoring were the only sounds. The tranquility was shattered when the radio crackled to life. Adventist was the battalion's call sign. C-Battery was Adventist 63, and this is how the transmission went:

"Adventist 63.   Coyote 7. Over."

"Coyote 7.   Adventist 63. Over."

"Adventist 63.   Coyote 7. Be advised we're closing in on your problem. Over."

"Coyote 7.   Adventist 63. Roger. Standing by. Over."

The bunker was now alive. I snapped shut my book. Kornowski swapped out his letter for the most recent MET and some slide-rules. With a start, Murphy woke up and ran outside for some air. Garfield nearly fell out of his chair and stood by his map table. Lt. Briggs flew down the stairs informing us the Captain was coming over and the Battalion CO, Colonel Barnes was on his way up, not expecting the artillery duel that would ensue.

Could this be the day we end this? At least for a while.

We were at the ready.

After their ride from Dong Ha, Colonel Barnes stepped into the bunker with his driver. More brass from headquarters had to wait in the OR. Sofian ran over to make sure the generator was gassed up and squeezed into the FDC bunker with us. The place was packed and everyone smoked while we waited.

The radio squawked:

"Adventist 63.   This is Coyote 7. Over."

"Coyote 7.   Adventist 63. Over."

"Adventist 63.   Coyote 7. FIRE MISSION! Over."

"Roger Coyote 7.   Adventist 63. Fire mission. Over."

"Adventist 63.   Coyote 7. 156 niner. Over."

"Coyote 7.   Adventist 63. 156 niner. Over."

"Adventist 63.   7 here. 1611. Over."

"Coyote 7.   Adventist 63. Say again. Over."

"Adventist 63.   Coyote 7. 1611. Over."

"Coyote 7.   Adventist 63. Roger, 1611. Over."

The target is plotted on the map, calculated, numbers sent to one gun and then . . .

KABAAM!

"Adventist 63.   Coyote 7. Drop 200. Over."

"Coyote 7.   Adventist 63. Drop 200. Over."

We had eyes on the ground in this battle, which was to our advantage in a big way. Our guns could edge closer and closer to the target as the FO adjusted our fire. The NVA were firing blindly into the grid their observer established weeks ago. Once we were on to them, the North Vietnamese were no longer trying to surprise us with random fire. They began peppering the base as fast as their cannons could fire, hoping to knock us out before their doom.

Three enemy rounds screamed into C-1 all at once.

The new numbers are relayed to the guns on the landline, and another 175 adjusts.

KABAAM!

Three more from across the Z land inside the wire.

"Adventist 63.   Coyote here. Getting close. Add 100. Over."

"Coyote 7.   Adventist 63. Roger. Add 100. Over."

One more shift.

KABAAM!

They were now firing at us one at a time, as fast as they could reload.

"Adventist 63.   This is Coyote 7. Fire at will! Over."

"Coyote 7.   Adventist 63. Affirmative, fire at will. Over."

KABAAM!   KABAAM!   KABAAM!

There were a few more adjustments as our 175 barrels got hot while the three crews hustled to keep up with our advisory. When their guns were silent, our boys lowered the big smoking tubes and sat down to have one of their own.

Colonel Barnes shook hands with Captain Gerber, our new CO, replacing Captain Tobiason, and motored in a small convoy back to Dong Ha in relative ease.

This was without a doubt the most exciting day for us so far. The brass was present, we were firing at them, and they were shooting back at us. We received more incoming in one hour than we had in two days, making this a wild one for everyone. This was much different than shooting at a pin on the map and maybe hearing about it later. Most of the time the forward observers let us know when our guns hit the targets, but this was the first time those targets were shooting back at us.

Some of our bunkers had been hit, but they weren't penetrated. The NVA's objective was to knock out the guns so their projectiles weren't set for fuse delay. With the delayed timer, a

Soldier By Chance

bunker would be obliterated and a 175 would jump off the ground. Most of the time they missed and the subterranean blast would blow rocks and dirt around, but the majority of the dangerous shrapnel was trapped beneath the earth. It was now "game on" and the chunks of iron from their projos could fly for a hundred feet in all directions. One of the three remaining guns was damaged, but repairable and a member of its crew was injured. The Marine Corpsman next door patched him up. Our mess tent was in tatters, however, part of the kitchen survived along with cases of hot dogs and sauerkraut. Some of the bunkers took direct hits, of course, requiring more sandbags to repair them. The outhouse didn't have a mark on it. I'm sure it was empty during that hour. Chunks of steal littered our camp and we kept finding them until we left the base.

The siege was over. The bunkers emptied. We all congratulated each other as if Charlie Battery had just won the war.

David Garfield takes a break

Kellerman returned the next morning. The laid-back Texan calmly told us about the previous night's ambush that killed two Marines on his patrol. He was the first in our Battery to fire his M-16 at the enemy.

Captain Gerber took command when we moved to C-1. He was a strong and fair commander with just enough of a sense of humor to make it impossible not to like him. You could tell right away he was one of those officers who genuinely cared about his men and he showed it the first real chance he got, which was now. After receiving the necessary supplies we would need to operate; ammunition, water, and food, the captain had steaks, beer, and ice trucked up from Dong Ha. Let the good times roll.

It took a few days for everyone to take a shower and some didn't bother, but we were clean, well-fed, and back to work without diving into the bunkers every hour. It was 120 degrees again and when I stood beneath the full 55-gallon drum and took my shower, I didn't want it to ever end.

DENTIST

I had been scheduled to go to the dentist in Dong Ha midway through our daily bombardment. A few days after the artillery in North Vietnam was hopefully destroyed, Private Jenkins, a new man, woke me up from a sound sleep. I looked down on him from my upper bunk while he banged on it.

"You're White? Right?"

"I think so. What's up?"

"I'm supposed to take you to the dentist in Dong Ha."

"What the . . . Now?"

He just stood there as I climbed down from the bunk and scratched my head for a second. Some of the sleeping men grunted their disapproval for the intrusion.

"Can we eat breakfast first?"

"Well, I hope so. I was sure countin' on it."

He actually giggled while climbing up the ladder for some chow.

For a new guy, Jenkins was a happy man. We were still sleeping with our boots on so it didn't take long to get my gear and leave the stinky bunker to meet him in the new Mess tent. This was the beginning of his tour as a truck driver for Motor Pool. His duty for the day was to drop me off at the Marine dentist in Dong Ha before picking up supplies.

The end of the siege allowed boxes of canned food to arrive. The big cans of hotdogs and sauerkraut were hidden behind cases of powdered eggs and cans of creamed corn, peas, carrots, and other tasty delights. Without refrigeration, frozen pork chops and other perishables would arrive every three or four days. Occasionally, cold milk would be waiting at breakfast.

While indulging in another hearty meal of "shit on a shingle," creamed hamburger on a piece of toast, Corporal Starkwell sat down with some of the replacements for the wounded men on Sergeant Bird's destroyed gun. Billy Starkwell was about to become an acting sergeant replacing Bird on a brand new 175. Two of his new men were riding to Dong Ha in Dougherty's truck, one of the original members of Charlie Battery. Starkwell introduced the new guys and told us to look out for them. After breakfast and lots of coffee, I climbed into Jenkins' deuce-and-a-half. Dougherty led the way in the 5-ton he was issued back in Oklahoma.

Mess Sergeant

I had never seen Jenkins or the other two men before. This would happen more often when we were transferred or went home. Half of Charlie battery would move to another part of the country before their year was up. There was no place left but south where everyone wanted to go because of better food, beer, whores, and although just as dangerous, no artillery incoming. It was necessary for new guys to infiltrate us so they could take over our jobs, creating a smooth transition.

We passed the crater where the ARVN bunker used to be before the visit from the Navy and left our gates for the six-mile trip to Dong Ha.

Private Jenkins was amazingly relaxed for someone so new in-country. I was wide-eyed and a little nervous my first week in Vietnam. Maybe the first month, maybe still. Most of us had been drafted, but he and a handful of others signed up for this, adding one year to their service.

Jenkins was a very funny man. I was looking forward to some news from home, but my driver had me in stitches while he told one joke after another.

Halfway to Dong Ha, Dougherty's truck hit a mine, lifting the front into the air and blasting it cockeyed, blocking the road. Jenkins shut up and slammed on the brakes as small arms fire strafed us. One round went through the door and zinged above my knees before crashing into the metal dashboard. Another went through the outer shell of the door and ricocheted around inside.

FUCK!

Every weapon has a distinct sound and these were AK-47s. Maybe five or six shooting at us from the right side of the road. Jenkins flew out the driver's door with me right behind him. We worked our way towards the other truck through the scrubby brush, which also concealed our attackers as they continued firing on the lead truck.

I opened the door and could see that Dougherty and his passengers were hurt. All were unconscious, but the legs on the guy on the right were mangled and bleeding from something that blew through the floor. As more AK fire was directed under the truck at my legs, I slammed the door and retreated to the roadside brush with Jenkins. The enemy hadn't unleashed a Rocket Propelled Grenade Launcher (RPG) and I sure as hell hoped they didn't have one.

Five-tons are built like a tank, well, almost. Pulling the wounded men out of it into the open didn't seem like a good idea. That we would also be in the open may have played into my decision to stay put and defend the truck when they attacked us, especially since Jenkins jumped out without his weapon. I tried to convince him to go back and get it, but as he put it, "No Fucking Way!"

I thought about getting Dougherty's M-16 from his truck for Jenkins, but a few more had joined the others. Their bullets were zinging over our heads as we crouched below the side of the road. This was my bad. I should have grabbed it when I had the chance.

We waited for the attack that would surely come when as if from heaven, a large convoy came roaring up at full speed. The jeep in the lead knew something was amiss ahead and ordered a charge. Marines jumped from the back of the trucks setting up defensive positions, but the NVA had disappeared into the bush.

Jenkins and I got our wounded out of Dougherty's truck and laid them on the side of the road. Dougherty could sit up but didn't know who or where he was. His eyes, nose, and ears were bleeding. The man in the middle was much the same, but the guy by the door was in dire straits. A Corpsman from the convoy injected him with a morphine popper when he came-to for a moment. He tried his best to help our new guy, but he was bleeding out. They called for a medevac to intercept the convoy to Dong Ha, but it was clear that this soldier wasn't going to make it.

Our two outside rear tires were shot up and the side was pockmarked with holes, but it ran. We drove it to the side to let one of their five-tons push Dougherty's off the road so they could pass.

We helped load our three wounded men into one of their trucks to take them to the hospital in Dong Ha, hoping the new man would make it. He did not. This was the second man I had just met who would end up on the wall in Washington and I didn't even know their names. The Marine Major in the jeep who had saved our ass ordered us back to our base with one of their trucks to accompany us. He also left a truckload of infantry to stay with our crippled five-ton until it could be retrieved before dark.

We were lucky that the bad guys weren't on both sides of the road or we would have easily been picked off. The Cavalry's arrival sealed the deal with our survival.

Jenkins told no jokes and was pale as he drove us back to camp. I was starting to get rattled when we left and halfway there, was a mess. It dawned on me that without the Marines, we wouldn't have stood a chance.

The flat tires went thubba-thubba-thubba up Highway 1 before one popped off, jolting me to another realization. Our lighter deuce-and-a-half would have been blown off the road and Jenkins and I would be toast.

The big guns were busy when the wounded truck limped into base. Some of the vehicles including our APC were in Dong Ha. Much safer there from incoming. Jenkins' shot-up truck, Dougherty's destroyed one, Westmoreland's 5-ton, a few jeeps, and the ammo tenders for the guns were the only vehicles that stayed up here.

We reported to Captain Gerber who clicked his pen for a while, shook his head, and told me to get back to work. Jenkins was ordered to change the tires on his truck whether it would run again or not.

Soldier By Chance

Sergeant Starkwell ran in after hearing about our ambush. I told him the same account I gave the Captain, remembering his request to watch out for his men. Billy looked at me with kind eyes and said, "Hitting a mine is like getting struck by lightning. There ain't much you can do about it." The CO told him to borrow a man from Horner's gun to help man his new 175.

The Captain would now have to secure another 5-ton and arrange for the removal of the shot up one on the side of the road. He would also have to replace the three men, two of them brand spanking new in-country. Dougherty's experience would be missed, but losing another man would weigh heaviest on Captain Gerber.

My friends on shift in the FDC bunker were busy supplying the guns with information. Hopefully they'd blow something else but dirt to smithereens. The off-duty crew would be at work in a few hours, but were now sound asleep. I quietly climbed up to my bunk for some rest, realistically knowing my thoughts would run wild recalling the trip to the dentist.

I didn't see the men on the other side of the road that were trying to kill us, but I could hear them yelling at each other. This was much more personal compared to the long-distance war we were involved in. The frantic high-pitched voices of our attackers stayed with me long into the night before I dozed off.

Have I not hideous death within my view,

Retaining but a quantity of life, which bleeds

Away, even as a form of wax, Resolveth

From his figure against the fire?

William Shakespeare, *King John*

I dreamed about the first day I reported to the Army in Oakland. Before being sworn in, a Marine Sergeant yelled out to fifty of us waiting to fly to Fort Lewis Washington for basic training. "Anyone want to be a Marine?" My fingers twitched, but I restrained my hand from going up. Something I would seldom do again. As we were boarding the bus to the airport, four were picked out of the line randomly, and instead of flying to Fort Lewis, they were on their way to the Camp Pendleton Marine base.

The 8th & the 4th was stationed in the First Corps Tactical Zone, or I-Corps, the northern of the four military sections in Vietnam. The 105 Battery in Quang Tri was the only other Army unit we had seen up there so far. Other than those guys, all were Marines. Some of our equipment was handed down to them as the Army upgraded, like my flak jacket. They still had jeeps from the Korean War as well as some of their artillery pieces. Most Marines were volunteers, the opposite of the Army. It was just assumed they would buck up to stronger discipline and more bullshit. They're designed to be a frontline army, the ones to hit the beach and storm the castle. Vietnam was an unusual war without a clear plan for victory in the midst of a large population whose loyalty was uncertain.

The Marines in I-Corps went on patrol like the southern forces and also protected fire installations. However, the Charlie and the Alpha bases under their watch along the DMZ had the distinguished privilege of receiving artillery incoming from North Vietnam. The 175 was not in the Marine's arsenal or Charlie Battery would not be sharing that privilege.

My father was a great storyteller. I had grown up listening to his war stories at cocktail parties while I was in the shadows down the hall. When I was a kid, the best pastime of all was playing war. After dividing sides and choosing from an array of weapons, including Roy Rogers six guns, and my favorite, a plastic Thomson machine gun, the play began. You slid the lever back and got ten seconds of Rat-tat-tat! We would kill each other over and over for hours. Oh, the joy of storming the machine gun nest, and after being hit countless times, tumbling and rolling on the grass in agonizing death.

My Cub Scout pack sat in the bleachers of the Saturday morning Fireman Frank Show in San Francisco while he drank beer during the cartoons. He asked each one of us personal questions. My turn was next and I couldn't wait for Micky Mouse to end so I could tell the slightly drunk fireman what I wanted to be when I grew up, "the armored force in the Army." As I got older, that desire gradually waned and the thought of war wasn't as attractive.

It was the killing and dying part that wasn't appealing. However, those are the elements that actually make it most exciting. There were a lot of us that couldn't get enough of it and kept coming back for more.

The crapshoot of life had sent me to Fort Lewis instead of Camp Pendleton where I would have been destined to be in the infantry. If I was tough enough to kick the shit out of anyone who made fun of "Flower Man," I know I would have gotten into it and perhaps become a different person. Once you are thrown into that mix, it doesn't matter if you believed in the war or not. You're fighting for yourself and the men next to you. Don't get me wrong. I fulfilled my duties and volunteered for more of them. I was also prepared to fight to the death with the men *next to me*. It wasn't likely to happen. Our war experience was just . . . well . . . different. Other than skirmishes on the perimeter, we rarely saw the enemy. They shot at us, and we shot at them across a great distance. The Marine and Army infantry fought an entirely different kind of war than we did. Although I feel lucky at how things turned out for me, I never met a Jarhead who wasn't proud of it. There are no ex-Marines, even if you are dead.

LAUNDRY DETAIL

I was eating a great breakfast of real eggs, real bacon, and real milk in the casual atmosphere that had overcome our camp after the siege, when Westmoreland found me to tag along on another run for sandbags. This time it was by the book: two trucks and two guards outside the village. We parked a quarter mile away and the perpetual crowd of thirty started filling them.

I was having a smoke, talking to Westmoreland and Bunge, the other guard, when someone tugged on my flak jacket. It was Huang On's little brother, who recognized me. He had stayed behind his dad that day in the Ville, watching me intently. I didn't notice it then, but now I could see he walked with a distinct limp. He told me he was wounded when our jets bombed their farm. The little guy carried a satchel full of Jack Daniels or Vietnamese wine. They would saw the bottoms of the bottles off, fill them with their own *whatever*, and glue them back on, leaving the government seal on the cap intact. He also had a pile of marijuana ten packs in his bag. I gave him some MPCs for a few of his bundles. We didn't have greenbacks in Vietnam. The Armed Services printed their own Military Payment Certificates. We got these on payday, the same day many of the men lost them in the monthly poker game.

Speaking very good English, he told me his mom and dad talked about my visit with his brother. All was good with his family. Huang On was in Hue at the University. His stepmother was as feisty as ever and Papa San was cashing in on the Black Market.

Turns out Papa was the honcho of the village. *Number One*, as his young son proudly described him. He told me the goods in his bag would gladly be exchanged for C-rations.

I wished him well and the little guy walked over to see if Bunge was interested in any of the stuff in his bag. We drove back to base with two trucks full of sandbags that I would help unload and stack around or on top of something.

It's a mystery to me how this village could have a laundry capable of serving the three different companies of C-1, the Marines, ARVN, and us. They wash, starch, and iron everything in your duffle bag with a purple tag stapled to each piece with your name on it. All without electricity!

Soldier By Chance

Ben Kazazowitz from the orderly room had been driving Lt. McCreedy's jeep once a week to the laundry outside our gate. I think Ben was getting a little spooked and refused to leave the compound. Kibisky's good instincts told him this might be the detail for me. He let me know and I ran to the OR to offer my assistance. Captain Gerber wasn't surprised to see me.

"Let me guess, are you volunteering to leave us again, Private White?"

"Just to take the laundry to the village, sir."

"You know, sleep is good, White."

"It's overrated, sir, and clean laundry is good, too . . . sir."

Captain Gerber frowned at me. "McCreedy's in Da Nang. Take his jeep. That will be all, Private."

"Yes, sir."

Makeshift village next door to C-1

I drove out the gates with a butt-load of duffle bags to the Vietnamese laundry. I paid a wad of MPCs for our clean clothes and sped over to my friends on the other side of the village. The industrious villagers had cleaned up the destruction from our Navy air attack; there was no sign of it.

By the time I climbed out of McCreedy's jeep, the plywood door flew open and little brother came out to greet me. After our siege, cases of C-rations had been accumulating in the mess tent to prevent the shortage we just experienced. I threw one in the jeep with the laundry. Little brother carried it into the hooch and set it on the mahogany table in front of his dad who stood and offered me a seat. Mama San brought Jack Daniels to the table. After explaining that I was on-duty and driving the lieutenant's jeep with the laundry, I told her I shouldn't stay long and had better refrain this time. She removed the libations displaying her bright red teeth and scurried to the other room. I'm not sure how many boxes of C-rations are in a case. Probably a dozen. A variety of three or four canned meats including ham and "mother fuckers" shared a box with crackers and cheese, packs of coffee, sugar, creamer, toilet paper, P-38 can opener, cigarettes, and a Sterno tab to heat your ham and mother fuckers. A lot of this stuff went into the trash, but every bit of it would be used by these people.

More than pleased, Papa San left the room and returned with four quarts of Jack Daniels and a pile of ten packs. I stared at the collection of mind-altering goods on the table. The vision of a drunk and stoned Charlie Battery responding to a ground attack wasn't pretty, and I didn't want to be responsible for such an event. This brief moment of clarity may have served all of us well. To many back in the battery, it would have been a brief moment of insanity. I thanked him and decided to leave empty-handed.

I rose from the table, anxious to get back. They agreed that I shouldn't stay long and followed me to the jeep. A group of neighbors and kids joined Huang On's family, creating a cluster of waving hands as I departed.

The mud at C-1 had turned to dust for a while. Probably a short one. We were almost at full complement with Billy Starkwell's new gun in action. Five men would complete our numbers. Dougherty and the wounded cannoneers positions were yet to be filled, but the crews had adjusted.

As usual, our fire missions were supporting the Alpha bases and activity across the DMZ, spotted from the air or forward observers. Khe Sanh was out of our range, but we could fire on enemy involvement northeast of the base that was now under siege.

Our camp was secure for the moment, allowing us to enjoy a good Christmas dinner, with turkey no less. The abundance of holiday mail put a smile on most of the men as we went about our business. On New Years' 1968, the focus of our fire was directed at Con Tien, which was under a major attack both on the ground and with artillery. The NVA must have suffered massive casualties during their attacks, with every firebase within range pounding them. Marine Jets joined in to drop 500 pounders and helicopter gunships swarmed into their ranks with rockets and machine guns. This wasn't the thick green jungle that spread over much of Vietnam. Cover here was at a minimum.

AUSTRALIA

One night at dinner, Specialist Kibisky told me to get ready for R&R first thing in the morning. Kibisky was usually the bearer of good news. Back in the bunker, I pulled my khaki uniform and some civilian clothes out of the duffle bag that was wedged in the corner of my bunk. Wrinkled but clean, I would wear my khakis all the way to Australia.

Rest and Recuperation was a mini-vacation that we got once during our tour in either Bangkok, Hong Kong, Taipei, Singapore, or Sydney. You were flown to one of the cities and cut loose for five days.

The next day, Jenkins was my driver in his repaired deuce-and-a-half still riddled with holes. He was proud driving that battle-hardened truck and his sense of humor suffered no injury as three jokes were under his belt by the time a small convoy had gathered for another trip to Dong Ha. We shared a moment of silence and relief as we passed the location of our ambush. He dropped me off at the Dong Ha airbase and I waited for a flight to Da Nang.

I loved riding in C-130s. Designed for short runways, the big cargo planes take off and almost go straight up. We landed at the airport and spent the night. Next morning in our khaki uniforms, a commercial 707 leaves Da Nang en route to Sidney with a planeload of vacationers and *stewardesses*! I was shocked at how this aspect of life was a distant memory. Well, not forgotten, as the Vietnamese women filling our sandbags, chewing the leaves and seeds of the betel palm, didn't allow my mind to wander in that direction. But now, it was a different story.

If I made it home and the odds were good . . . I could smell and feel the soft skin of a woman. I could touch her and she . . . Oh Fuck, I was getting a hard-on. Down, boy, there's plenty of time for that later. All of a sudden, I was very anxious for that time.

A lot of us had a short timer's calendar. We marked off every day and were left with the exact number of days remaining on our tour. At times, when you met someone, that was the first thing you learned about him. Some of the men on the plane were sharing the number of days they had remaining in-country.

Soldier By Chance

"Hi, Jack Bennet, 177 days." This tradition just seemed more frustrating to me. I had a rough idea when the day would come, because Kibisky would let me know. I settled into my seat and decided to stick with that plan.

As we flew over Australia, I started to get worried about my five-day R&R. It seemed as if it was taking forever to fly over the continent, and we had to come back. Not a lot of green in this part of Australia. Red dirt and rough desert that was endless.

Sydney was a very clean and pretty city surrounding a beautiful harbor with beaches close by. It also had a famous bridge crossing the bay, reminding me of another place back home. I wanted to take some pictures, but had lost my camera in Da Nang.

I sat next to another Marine Supply Sergeant on the flight from Da Nang. We got rooms in a small hotel and explored the city for a few days together. We met early on the first morning and took a train to a beach not far away. Hot summer day, beautiful beach, waves to body surf, and pretty girls. From mud and bombs, to this. What a glorious day!

I don't know what they ate that was any different, but these were some healthy people. They were strong with broad shoulders and the women had big breasts. After six months in the backwoods of Vietnam, I could have concocted the big boobs in my mind.

When in uniform, I could not pay for a beer. Australia also had a contingent of forces supporting us, but we never crossed paths in Vietnam.

I did fall in love with a sweet girl from Sydney. We met on the street one night in front of my hotel. She held my hand and took me to a house nearby where a really big chain-smoking woman was sitting at a small desk watching the telly. I paid her twenty bucks and I can't believe I forgot her name. Anyway, we went into a tiny room with a bed. This was the weirdest sex I ever had. A man came in with a delivery of some kind and my girlfriend recognized his voice. She opened the curtain with her foot and started talking to this guy she knew from high school. During their conversation about the good old days, she started complaining that I was taking too much time. I kissed her goodbye and promised to write.

This was my first and only time with a prostitute. On the Z, we were never close to any. No milk, no beer, no girls. Once was enough.

The day after my romantic encounter, I was having breakfast with some of the others on R&R, reading the paper trying to catch up on the world. The Australian paper was describing some of the early events of what would become known as the "Tet Offensive." I had no idea how we were faring up there; the attacks on the larger bases dominated the news. Interestingly, I was with my new friends when we found out about Tet.

There were mixed emotions about it. My first reaction was an urge to get back to my unit, but who wants to leave a beach full of beautiful women for the drudgery of war in someone else's country?

North Vietnam had been sneaking men and supplies into the south for some time, preparing for the Tet Offensive. For every man we killed on the Ho Chi Minh Trail, two managed to make their way into South Vietnam armed to the teeth. They waited outside almost every American military base for the lunar holiday, beginning on the first new moon after January 20th. A cease fire during this time allowed the ARVN soldiers to go home to celebrate, and our forces to relax for a few days. On January 30, 1968, they attacked us with a vengeance, inflicting serious casualties and damage. Their goal of ending the war with a fatal blow didn't materialize and thousands were lost in the attempt. Initially we felt victorious, but the tide had turned. The anti-war movement in the U.S. now had a full head of steam, and the resolve of our enemy was only strengthened.

DARWIN

Our vacation was over, almost. The 707 taking us back to a land in chaos, broke down, we were told. After landing on the top of Australia at Darwin, it would take three days for another plane to retrieve us. In the meantime, our planeload of GIs got to run amok in that Aussie town.

We were bused to an Australian Air Force base and assigned to a large barracks for all of us. We ate our meals in the Air Force Mess Hall and most everyone remained on the base, but we could go anywhere, so I did. It was difficult to run amok in Darwin in those early days of 1968. Most of the shops were closed or empty, perhaps because of the intense heat, being so close to the equator. A small grocery with slim pick'ins was open. Dusty *Life* magazines over six months old lay on the counter next to cases of warm beer. A huge beer hall capable of seating a hundred or more was across the street.

Some of us spent the super-hot afternoons under cover at the beer hall. The establishment had fifty or more card tables with rusty folding chairs. There were no sides to the structure, just a metal roof to supply shade from the blistering sun and a shield to hold off the torrential rains.

Aborigines were the main patrons in the afternoons, actually, more than likely, all day. Alcohol was not their friend. They were falling off the rusty chairs and staggering about almost blindly. I seldom saw the women vacate their seats as most of them were passed out with their heads on the table. It appeared they were less adept at drinking than the men who could hardly stand up.

I was facing the urinal when a young Aboriginal staggered in and while he was pissing away, he accidentally bumped against me. He was dead sure I was going to beat the hell out of him as he cowered against the wall.

On the afternoon of the third day, I was with a couple of men from the grounded plane when all of us got hungry at the same time. The three of us had been hanging out drinking beer all afternoon and were starting to blend in with the Aborigines. Before we could leave, a truckload of blokes busted in the place to down a few beers and after seeing our uniforms, a full tray arrived at our table. We were hungry, but more beer was okay. They pulled up some chairs and wanted to know everything about the war. All of us had different stories to tell and we enjoyed their company. They gave us a boost with their incredible energy.

They were on their way to a big party on a ranch outside of town and invited us to go along. I was up for it, but my two mates were going back to the base for dinner. I got in the back of a beat-up 1950 Chevy pickup with them and we arrived after dark. This was a big party, a least a hundred. I was the only Yank and they treated me like a celebrity.

There were big tubs of ice filled with bottles of beer everywhere. Australia makes really good beer. It also makes very tough people. After downing a few, I was drawn to a commotion not far away with quite a bit of yelling and screaming. At first, I thought it was a cockfight with fifty people encircling it. A cockfight it wasn't; exactly the opposite. There were two large-breasted women beating the crap out of each other, knocking themselves senseless. I've watched fights and been in some, but this bout was off the charts. They punched, clawed, and kicked, egged on by the yelling of the crowd. Finally, someone stepped in and a few more helped separate the combatants. A little late. Their faces were swollen and covered in blood. Someone picked up a tooth and held it up to the cheers of the onlookers. This party showed no signs of ever ending. I hitched a ride back to the base and arrived as the sun was coming up, just in time to splash some water on my face and board the plane back to Southeast Asia.

BACK IN-COUNTRY

The information about Tet was sketchy. I did find out why it took three days to return on the same plane that supposedly broke down. The airport at Da Nang was for combat missions only, refueling and arming the Phantoms, F105s, Huey gunships, Puff the Magic Dragons, and anything else that could fly and spit out ordnance. The 707 would have to wait for the situation to calm down, which it had.

Approaching the Da Nang airport, we noticed scars of the offensive lining the edge of the runway with the wreckage of planes as crews hustled to repair divots here and there. Those of us heading north were transferred to another plane. As our C-130 circled the airport, it became clear that Dong Ha had suffered the same fate. I spent the night at the base until the road was cleared of mines and a big enough swath was opened by Navy Jets to allow reinforcements into C-1. My base was surrounded by an NVA regiment. I got a ride right to the gate with five truckloads of Marines beefing up our defenses.

After changing out of vacation clothes into more appropriate attire for the present situation, it was time to report in. On my way to the OR, a single round soared overhead landing inside the wire, taking out a few of our land mines with it.

The somewhat casual atmosphere I had left was now replaced by that tense gaze of men on alert. There wasn't much of a break between the artillery siege and this one on the ground. The First Sergeant was relaxed enough to ask how Australia was before informing me of our dangerous predicament and assigning me to guard duty.

Artillery was now supporting us from every firebase within range and two more Marine Companies arrived to defend the village next to us. We added four more M-60s to our perimeter; two on the north side to help defend the guns and the other two on the west pointing into the emptiness. Sandbags from the bunkers were hastily stacked around them. Sofian and I spent my first night back behind one.

I really liked Wayne Sofian. He had a lot of responsibility driving the APC and maintaining it and the generator. He also filled sandbags and worked in fire direction on my shift. Wayne didn't have time to volunteer for sandbag runs. Everyone in my section worked hard and performed their duties admirably. You could say that about all of Charlie Battery. The cooks busted butt to put three meals on the table, with some exceptions like when we were under siege. Motor Pool was constantly repairing and maintaining the twenty vehicles that were always in motion. The four-gun crews were at work all day and often all night. These were big cannons. Everything about them was big—the projectiles, the powder, and the vehicle that moved them around. The gun bunnies also spent more time in the monsoon rains with no cover and the gun pits quickly become mud pits.

Most of these men had been uprooted from their lives with a draft notice. It's pretty amazing when you think about it. I'm not saying everyone got along splendidly. There were numerous disagreements and some major assholes, but we all did our job.

Ordinarily, communication landlines would connect the machine gun nests with each other and headquarters, but because of the haste of our preparation, the only word we got came from the sergeant of the guard who made the rounds. Illumination flares from neighboring 105 and 155 batteries were now lighting up the land outside our wire.

"Puff the Magic Dragon" - Mini-Gun Ship

Since our arrival at Dong Ha, we couldn't help but watch the Gatling gun ships miles and miles away in the hills to the west. Various aircraft carried the guns but AC-47s or "Spooky's" were the platform of choice up here. The big planes had three guns on the left side. They would fly in a tight circle banked over so the mini-guns pointing earthward could shoot a hail of tracers, pulverizing their target. If you took time lapse pictures, they would create a perfect orange funnel pointing earthward. Now these gunships, "Puff the Magic Dragons," supported us not far beyond our perimeter.

Two of the four ammo carriers with their big machine guns were spread out behind us. Speaking softly, Sofian described to me the night Tet began, leading up to the present situation. There had been incoming during the day and perimeter skirmishes at night, but the main force had just arrived from the northwest. Our whispers fell silent when the hissing of the illumination flares and their glow eventually withered to nothing after landing on earth. These periods of utter silence and absolute blackness were short. During one of those moments, the void was shattered when some Marines on our right started yelling. Their machine guns opened up and a cluster of illumination rounds lit up the rolling hills in front of us. Every gun on the west side got hot plastering them. Sofian and I didn't see anybody out there, but we blasted away with the rest throughout the night if we thought anything moved. It's amazing what you think you see in the dark.

There were serious attempts on our perimeter, but artillery support, help from the sky, and the Marine Companies were enough to prevent our wire from being breached.

Next morning, our big guns were being repositioned to shoot in the opposite direction. Dong Ha was now surrounded by 4000 NVA and our 175s were lofting their projos right over us. I rummaged through my stuff looking for the earplugs we were issued at Fort Sill. Earlier, I got caught in front of one when she blew and my ears rang for weeks. To this day, my left one is only about fifty percent effective.

The search was on for the maps surrounding Dong Ha. We never thought our targets would be on the spot where Charlie Battery began to fight in this war.

The NVA around us moved south to join up with their comrades. Eventually, with more Marine infantry pouring in as well as Army helicopter gunships and every fire base in range pounding them, they drifted southwest to the A Shau Valley or dissipated into the western hills to join the siege around Khe Sanh.

The rains came to a halt and those bright 120-degree days returned along with the somewhat lazy period, much like what we had experienced in Quang Tri. The guns were frequently silent and most of the Marine infantry companies had moved out.

During this peaceful time, Ben wanted the laundry detail back. He said he was going stir crazy, but I wasn't going to let it go. This was the best assignment that I had ever volunteered for. I was feeling for Ben. I'd have to think about it.

The First Sergeant liked me for some reason. I think he felt guilty for assigning me to one of the guns on that rainy night back in Oklahoma. For whatever reason, he told Ben Kazazowitz to shove it.

One of the Connexes contained a bag of baseball equipment—mitts, bats, even bases, but no balls. We discovered this in Dong Ha when it calmed down enough to play ball. Meanwhile my dad had sent us two new softballs.

Captain Gerber had more cold beer sent up and the cooks put together burgers and potato salad. We set up a field behind the guns that were now facing north again and had an afternoon of burgers, beer, and baseball. It doesn't get any better than that.

I decided not to venture into the village for a while so as not to press my luck with the VC or Lieutenant McCreedy. The laundry was just outside our gates, whereas my friends were on the other side of the town. I was Ben's friend again after I handed the detail back to him. My visits out there were risky for me and for Huang On's family. I was hopeful that their celebration of Tet included Number One Son.

We had random fire missions and incoming from the North was also sporadic. There were those of us who had settled into our somewhat peaceful life at C-1, but the confines of our perimeter had others itching to move on.

Rumors were floating about an upcoming move south. The sandbag runs were over. My God, we had covered everything with them and then we covered everything again. I don't know where the artillery on the other side of the DMZ went, but they weren't pestering us.

All of our equipment showed the signs of the crashing and banging it had endured for the past nine months. Thousands of the 156-pound projectiles had spun their way out of the tubes. After three hundred rounds, with all three bags of powder, the whole barrel had to be exchanged for a new one. These are made from the highest-grade steel and you can imagine how precise the machining must be to bore a .175-millimeter hole through a thirty-three-foot block of steel and spin the rifling. All three batteries changed over three hundred gun tubes in the first year. In four years, they fired over a half million rounds of 175 and 8-inch ammunition.

The trucks in Motor Pool had to haul all this ammunition over rough terrain and the ammo carriers supplied the guns with it. If the First Sergeant had not assigned me to Corporal Horner's gun, I would have had the job of changing one hundred of our tubes. The hydraulics were constantly leaking, blowing lines from the enormous weight and concussion. The explosion required to push the big projectile through the tube for twenty-five miles exerted tremendous shock on the whole vehicle. Specialist Five Nelson was the lucky recipient of these duties.

After I returned to the U.S., Charlie Battery changed over to the 8-inch howitzer, the gun they would take to Con Tien when the Marines left Vietnam in 1969. The 8-inch was one of our most accurate artillery pieces during the war.

It was time for some major maintenance. Most of the battery saddled up for a land march back to Dong Ha. Horner and Sergeant Rollins needed new tubes, along with a complete overhaul. The cooks placed cases of C-rations at each occupied bunker for our last days at the base, then broke down the tents and packed all the mess equipment.

Two-gun crews would remain to conduct any fire missions sent our way by forward observers. Their ammo carriers held enough for our stay. In theory, the powder was stacked behind sandbags to prevent the whole place from lighting up. Sofian and Garfield would ride to Dong Ha with the guns to retrieve our command vehicle. Fire missions were still conducted from the bunker, but we started breaking everything down to transfer it back to the rig.

This is from a letter I sent home:

> *It's very lonely up here now, about fifty of us, thirty Marines and a lot of ARVN. At night, we don't have one man on the perimeter. Still, if an ARVN is caught within our area, he is yelled at and literally kicked out. Even the black Americans hate the "gooks." Here we are fighting for peace, yet it would take another J.C. to restore it amongst ourselves.*

Fire direction and two-gun crews were all that remained at our northern base after the convoy left for Dong Ha. Lieutenant Briggs sent me to the village for what laundry was left. Kazazowitz left with Kibisky and Desmond from the OR. I had talked my friend Jimmy Hobbs to go with me. He never understood why I went outside the wire for these details. We picked up our laundry, nothing to leave this time, and drove over to Huang On's house. I had to coax

Jimmy inside and he was very hesitant to sit down with me. Jack Daniels arrived via the ever so gracious step-mother. We all downed a glass and didn't decline another.

Little brother told me Huang On was there during TET but had gone back to Hue. The University was damaged and classes were cancelled. He went back to see who had survived the onslaught. We were surprised to learn that the whole village knew Charlie Battery was leaving our base before we did.

As Jimmy began to sense the bond with these people, he was anxious to go again. But that would never happen. There is something about a goodbye when it really is one. Little Brother held on to my leg and wouldn't let go as I was walking away. Even Mama San's perpetual smile was gone, closed lips concealing her red teeth. I shook Papa San's hand and we climbed into the Jeep. I was truly sad to drive away for the last time.

With the APC loaded and the two guns ready for travel, we left C-1. I would never forget this place.

HUE

Convoy departing Dong Ha for Hue

First Lieutenant Carpenter led the convoy back to our original camp to regroup with the rest of our unit. We spent a few days at the base we built months ago. It was much the same, but the FDC bunker was completed and the Seabees were beginning to build wooden barracks to replace the tents. The vehicles were serviced and we loaded up on supplies for our next assignment. This is where Howden left us to join another battery in the South. Howden was one of the smarter people I've known and a man of few words. He left us *without one*.

On the third morning, the whole battery was warming up waiting for the sun to rise. As soon as the early morning light provided enough to safely venture down Highway 1, we were underway. We had taken this route to Quang Tri months ago, but that was a ten-mile trip. Hue was fifty miles away and from there our journey would end in the mountains on the eastern edge of the A Shau Valley, the middle of nowhere. We were going to Hue, the provincial capital that Huang On hoped I could visit because of its ancient history and splendor. That was before Tet.

The convoy passed our old camp at Quang Tri; a Marine 8-inch battery occupied it now. From here on, this was new territory for me. I looked forward to every land march. We lived in bases surrounded by barbed wire, minefields, and machine guns. It never felt like it, but technically, it was much the same as a prison. My section and most of the battery never left the compounds until we moved to another. That long stretch of sand passed beyond our old camp for miles. It occurred to me that we might catch up with that man bouncing the tree trunk on his shoulder.

The white sand ended abruptly, spilling into a sea of green. There were small farms in the lush valleys filled with rice and everything else that would grow. A sweet smell filled the air, replacing the odor of cobalt and burnt powder inside the wire surrounding the Fire bases.

It's about fifty miles from Dong Ha to Hue. While I was with the guns sailing up the coast, the battalion motored up this road on their way to Dong Ha. We sped through the abundant valleys and came to a wide river where I saw the boat people. Nine months ago, David Garfield told me about them when he described the land march from Da Nang. Hundreds of Sampans filled the center of the river lashed together creating a floating city. There were restaurants, opium dens, bars, some sold chickens, pigs, fish, AK-47s, and rice. They had everything. You just walked from boat to boat and if hostilities erupted, they went somewhere else.

    This is how I would have chosen to live in this country. There was a sense of freedom about the lifestyle and a slight improvement in sanitary practices. After rolling up their pant leg and shitting over the side of the Sampan, the locals could splash water on their ass instead of leaving it be—one of the many reasons we NEVER drank water that wasn't green and smelled like bleach. Kellerman talked about filling plastic bottles with fresh water and selling them in stores when he got back to Dallas. We couldn't imagine paying for water back home, but in Vietnam it sure sounded good.

    We crossed the river and began climbing our way through gentle hills closing in on the old Capital. All of us knew that a whole lot of shit came down in Hue. The NVA and VC had finally been evicted after twenty-four days of brutal, old school, house to house fighting.

This was one of the only cities built by the old cultures left in South Vietnam. Stone temples and walkways curved through the hills around the ancient palaces. Back on that ill-advised sandbag run in the Ville outside C-1, Huang On gave me a picture of him sitting on one of these old walkways. On the back he wrote: "Thank you my American friend for helping my country."

The convoy wove its way through a valley that opened up looking down on the provincial capital in front of steep tropical hillsides. We drove down to the Perfume River and turned right in front of the main bridge, which was completely destroyed, and slowed to a crawl as the road followed the river directly across from the city. The visual signs of war were very evident along with the pungent odor of a myriad of recently detonated high explosives.

Hue was built by the Chinese in 1601. When Tet raged through "The Great Interior City," the Marines, Army, and ARVN were reluctant to use artillery or air strikes. In the end, they had no choice. The B-52s were called off, but we bombed the shit out of Hue. It was eighty percent destroyed and an equal percentage of its people were homeless or dead. I was reminded of Montecassino, that ancient abbey in Italy that we flattened in WWII with an armada of B-24s. The rubble created an ideal fortress to defend and the Germans held out for weeks inflicting enormous casualties on the Allied forces. The same was true in Hue, but instead of B-52s, we blasted it with conventional weapons. We passed in front of what was left of the Citadel on the way to the only intact bridge crossing the Perfume River. All the windows were shot or blown out of the buildings. Bullet holes covered every surface and black stains marked the walls and ground from explosions delivered by mortars, rockets, grenades thrown by hand or grenade launchers, RPGs, cannon fire, suicide sappers, and even flame throwers. This city witnessed some of the heaviest fighting of the war.

We hadn't gone far after crossing the river when the train of vehicles came to a stop on a wide part of the road. The Captain, First Sergeant, and Kibisky, along with some support, would stay here in a rear area while the rest of us made the mountainous trip to Bastogne. First Lieutenant Carpenter would also leave us to lead his own 175 battery in the central highlands. We would miss that fair and true officer. This was an especially difficult transition because the newly promoted First Lieutenant McCreedy would now be our executive officer, the man essentially in charge of Charlie Battery with the captain in the rear. Oh boy.

One of the many concrete bunkers left behind by the French after their retreat in 1954

BASTOGNE

Forward Fire Base Bastogne

We stretched our legs and every man in the convoy was issued bundles of bandoleers full of magazines for our M-16s. Ammo for the M-79 grenade launchers in our section went to Kornowski who loved that thing. Early chow at Dong Ha would tide us over until the diesels stopped idling in Bastogne. Staff Sergeant Breem went up and down the line advising us to get out our ponchos.

I climbed back on top of the APC and we began the bumpy fifteen-mile ride to the remote base. Kornowski and Hobbs got up there with me, but the rest of my section felt safer inside. I hated it in there and always rode on top. When three M-48 Patton tanks and some infantry armored personnel carriers with 50s on top joined the convoy interspersed throughout its ranks, we knew this was going to be a wild ride.

As we motored into the hills, they got larger and steeper with trees and vines covering the roadside. The recently excavated road may have been made to reach Bastogne.

When the mountainsides got really thick, the convoy cut loose. The tank cannons, 50s, and every weapon in the convoy blasted the rainforest all the way to the base. I tried to picture someone out there waiting to ambush us . . . but couldn't. I emptied twenty-five magazines into the hillsides on the way, some at full automatic and some target practicing. Kornowski exhausted our large supply of M-79 grenades while Jimmy leaned back and took it all in. He gave me some of his magazines and I blasted some more. There wasn't the slightest breeze and a mix of the pungent odor of spent explosives and diesel exhaust hung in the air.

I had never seen mountains like this. They were scoops of ice cream neatly stacked all the same size, covered with a one-hundred-foot canopy of rainforest. Halfway in, we found out why it was a rainforest and we couldn't get under our ponchos fast enough. The hot clear day was suddenly darkened by clouds that just appeared from out of nowhere. Then it rained for half an hour. I think that's what you call it. I'd never even imagined a deluge like that. During the monsoons, it rained for weeks on end. At Bastogne, we were flushed down the toilet every afternoon. A drop would hit the ground and within seconds, little creeks ran down the hills through the dust. A moment or two more and the dust was mud and after thirty minutes, it all came to an abrupt halt. Blue sky reappeared and it was over until the next day.

By the time our convoy rounded a hill and dropped into Bastogne, the rain had ceased as well as every weapon along for the ride. Before we left Hue, Bastogne was described as a "hellhole" and "a hard to defend position."

Construction of the base had begun in February of 1968, so it was far from complete. They had just expanded it to accommodate our 175s.

The 101st Airborne were the custodians of the base. Probably a battalion of infantry and mortar platoons. A large area in this wide valley had been cleared with the foliage like a one hundred-foot-tall fence on the edge. The Army Airborne had loaded the forest with Claymore mines, so it wasn't too easy to sneak around out there. They also took care of guarding the perimeter, which was substantial, replete with wire, mines, and machine guns. We moved into an area that had been previously occupied. Fire Direction worked in our APC with its tent and slept in another. The Lieutenants had their own tent looking out on Charlie Battery as it wove its way down the naked ravine surrounded by this lush rainforest.

With all of Charlie Battery's men and supplies unloaded, our trucks joined the tanks and APCs, and shot their way back to Hue. The road would become enemy territory for two weeks until the next convoy blasted their way back in.

Our mission here was to support the 1st Cavalry and 101st Airborne during operation Delaware. Our guns could reach the north end of the A Shau Valley, which was a nest of NVA. There were forward observers out there, but some of our outgoing was in response to motion sensors dropped from the air. FDC and the gun crews had to be at the ready to be effective. If we were, there was seldom any word about it.

Rocket and mortar attacks were the norm here. On April 30th, a heavy barrage of .132-mm rockets hit us. One of our 3/4-ton trucks took a direct hit and was blown apart. Ground assaults caused the most concern, however. For good reason, I might add. We could tell on our own that thousands of them could be completely hidden not far from our wire under this canopy. We would learn that the Army felt it could have been overrun at any time. I'm really glad I didn't know that. I found out years later that in 1972, it was completely overrun and occupied by the enemy. ARVN commando raids finally evicted them before they could set up artillery to shell Hue.

There were nightly skirmishes on the perimeter, mostly small arms and RPG fire. Luckily for us, the large army had spread out in the A Shau Valley, which was a direct pipeline to the Ho Chi Minh Trail. From there, they joined the attacks on Khe Sanh and the Alpha and Charlie bases in the North or headed south.

The rains continued. Let me rephrase that; every day, the afternoon deluge hit us at 3:20, give or take a few seconds. After it was finally over and the water dripping from the forest became a single drop, you could almost hear and watch more growth appear in the intense heat.

Bastogne was one of the most amazing places I had ever been or would be. This wasn't Yosemite or the Grand Canyon; it was the environment with the rain, the heat, and the soil. Everything was alive and multiplying before your eyes.

The bugs! My God, the bugs! Hundreds of them I'd never seen or heard of. The gun crews found a way to use them for their amusement, something we were short of out here. We didn't even get the military music channel on our transistor radios to the dismay of the country fans, which included most of Charlie Battery.

The centipedes were almost a foot long and the scorpions topped off about the size of a large mouse. Each crew picked their gladiator and put them in a ring together, betting on the outcome, like a cockfight with fifty men yelling and throwing money into a hat. These combatants fed on insects and frogs. Watching a centipede devour a frog was pure entertainment.

One morning I was awakened by something wiggling at my feet. In spite of the hot days, the nights were cold at our elevation, so we were tucked in our recently cleaned sleeping bags. If we knew better, we would have been sleeping with our boots on, however, it was refreshing not to hit the rack in uniform. I didn't move a muscle as something crawled up my leg and knowing exactly what it was, felt the hundred prickly legs as it worked its way up my chest. The little monster hung a left as it scurried under my chin, across my shoulder, and out the bag. I gave the creature to Sergeant Horner's gun.

The centipedes had the upper hand in the beginning of the matches, but eventually the persistent stings from the scorpion would declare him a winner. This proved to be the case too often, so in spite of trying to find bigger centipedes, the bouts subsided and were soon history.

For some reason, McCreedy really took pleasure in teaching the new boys that he was an asshole. His own driver messed up and the lieutenant had him dig a hole ten inches in diameter, over eight feet deep with a posthole digger. He had to start right after the daily deluge and work until dinner. After tying ropes on the handles to get deep enough, it took him two weeks to finish. Lieutenant McCreedy sat in a chair harassing him to make it more insulting.

I did some exploring and came across a small abandoned bunker. There were cots left behind that I liberated. Jimmy Hobbs and I lugged down the hill some four-foot culvert halves that the Airborne guys next door had given me. A pond sat in the ravine right below the spot where I would build a small bunker. I used the 175 powder boxes and made walls four feet high on three sides and Jimmy helped me set the culvert halves on top. Then of course, I covered the whole thing with sandbags. My friends couldn't believe I would fill more sandbags without being ordered. With the legs cut off one of the cots, it fit on top of the walls while the other had room to spare below. A couple of pallets made a nice deck in front above the pond.

If I was off duty during the daily deluge, lying in my cot watching the pond overflow became my favorite pastime. Simple pleasures.

Hobbs was an artist. I mention his chosen profession to indicate his lack of desire to bust his butt. Not that he didn't, when necessary, always fulfilling his duties in FDC as one of the top men with Kornowski since Howden's departure. He also outranked me. But aside from helping with the culvert halves, he sat on his ass and read or watched as I built the bunker. I knew Jimmy by now and didn't mind. It was my idea to build it to get out of the stinking, hot tent and I was glad he was my friend.

The guns were shooting at motion detectors miles and miles away over a dense jungle. There were fire missions in the A Shau Valley with forward observers, but for the most part, we had no idea what was going on around us.

Other than our shift in fire direction, we didn't have much to do, with no guard duty or sandbags to fill. McCreedy even stopped inventing meaningless details to fuck with us. Rockets and mortars came in, but the forest was so thick, their Forward Observers would have to weave between the Claymores to direct fire. They just hit us helter-skelter.

Bastogne was very isolated. Choppers came daily, and every two weeks the convoy blasted its way in with a hail of firepower. We could hear them coming hours away.

The boys in my squad were running out of supplies like toothpaste, razor blades, cigarettes, and deodorant. I should have tried it. The smell I ditched in Australia had returned with a vengeance. Honestly, though, the guys who rolled it under their pits didn't smell all that great. Without showers, they stank even more.

When it was time to resupply, it was just assumed that I would be the one to get them. The men in my section made it clear that without a convoy, they were staying put. With a long list and a wad of MPCs, I walked down to the LZ to wait for a chopper. It didn't take long. I saluted a Colonel and more of the brass arriving for the 101st and stepped aboard the Huey bound for Hue. I loved flying in these things. The door gunner said hello as I leaned against the back wall next to him. This was another fun ride, flying at a hundred miles an hour, twenty feet above the rolling treetops, around the hills and through the valleys, banking back and forth. When the chopper made a sharp left turn, the trees whisking by almost slapped you in the face and instantly blue sky filled the whole picture. There was a reason for flying like this. By the time the enemy could get a bead on you, the chopper was gone. There were a few rivers, or perhaps one, snaking back and forth. As we made our way to Hue, the forest was amazing, unlike anything I had seen or imagined. I filled all the orders and was back in Bastogne for dinner.

That night, Lieutenant Briggs informed me of my promotion to E-4. McCreedy should have been the one to deliver the news, but we had been at odds for some time. I was glad it was Briggs. It took a while, but the gung-ho attitude I had started out with was waning. I was one of only three in my basic training company to earn a stripe, but I was beginning to think that this war was doing more harm than good. The Vietnamese in power and the U.S. were hellbent on defeating the Communists, but the people just wanted to get on with their lives. If we had to destroy this country to get rid of the Commies, well holy shit! It made no sense!

While off duty one afternoon, I was sitting on my cot reading *The Tempest*. As I've mentioned, a large volume of the *Complete Works of William Shakespeare* had accompanied me since Oakland. It was a pain in the ass to lug around, but was destined to be finished.

I heard a mini-whistle and looked up to see a small ball of orange light and a rain of shrapnel with a bang across the pond.

MORTAR! Two more edged their way up the draw and that was it. I was so accustomed to the big guns, I didn't even flinch.

A germ can kill you . . . If a fourth round had worked its way up the ravine, it would have ended me. Rockets also flew into Bastogne with another unique sound. They had a sharp explosion, unlike the more concussive bangs from artillery.

We bathed in a small river once a month before the afternoon deluge. All of the ice cream scoops had rivers running between them. After disarming some Claymores to get through the perimeter, a large group would leave the compound with men on the flanks and walk down to the river. One half stood guard, while the rest took their bath at Bastogne. We would walk into the water fully clothed, boots on, with a bar of soap, and wash our uniform first, hang it on some bushes, and wash ourselves. By the time we were somewhat clean, the uniforms were almost dry. Perfect, get in your boots, flak jacket, helmet, and pick up your weapon to stand guard as the other half takes their bath. After the walk up the hill in the heat, our uniforms were as wet as when they came out of the river and the afternoon dump had yet to begin.

NAPALM

B-52s pounding North Vietnam as seen from Dong Ha

The most dramatic firepower we witnessed came from the sky. On day one in Dong Ha we could see the B-52 raids in the DMZ. Black clouds rocketed a thousand feet high, one after another, as the big jets dropped their loads at great speed. Then our Navy released four, five hundred-pounders on C-1. At Bastogne, we got to watch the trifecta of destructive power—napalm.

One morning, there was what sounded like a typical response to a skirmish on our perimeter. After fifteen minutes of back and forth small arms fire, the roar of a jet directly overhead scared the hell out of me. By the time I saw the F-4 Phantom, two large canisters were tumbling towards the forest barricade on the western edge. Anything there was instantly incinerated by a huge ball of fire that kept burning and burning. Then a second Phantom's canisters landed above the Army Airborne camp. Less than a week later, we didn't hear an attack of any kind or the two F-105 Thunder Chiefs when their four firebombs scorched another piece of Vietnamese real estate outside our wire. Burnt napalm leaves behind a horrible smell that wouldn't leave us until the daily rainfall gradually washed it away. It smelled like a mix of burning gasoline and a weird chemical. We blew up the jungles of Vietnam by conventional means - explosives and Napalm—but there were more effective ways to expose the enemy.

Associated Press

AGENT ORANGE

Defense Government News Photo

Before the next convoy shot its way into Bastogne, every living thing but us would be dead or dying. Standing in the mud waiting for breakfast one morning, three staggered C-130s lumbered their way towards us with huge clouds of orange dust trailing them as they faded into the green maze. In three days, everything under their path was turning brown. After five days, the planes came back delivering more billowing orange powder from the bottom of the big transports as they made their way along the line of dying forest until the tanks of Agent Orange were empty, deep into Vietnam. Like mowing the lawn, but killing it. Before flying over us, they cut the flow trying to keep the crap out of our base, but it still made its way in. We had never heard of Agent Orange. This activity continued for weeks until a huge part of the forest around the base was poisoned. What was once a unique and amazing place, was now dead. The thriving jungle around Bastogne was its downfall. It provided too much cover, so we killed it.

The next convoy drove through a dead landscape on its way to re-supply us without blasting all the way in. We could hear them in the far distance, but once they entered the defoliated forest, their fire ceased and the diesel engines penetrated the quiet.

This worked in two ways. Because they were more exposed, the perimeter attacks subsided, and crawling through the orange dust must have also been a deterrent. When the generators weren't running, there were periods of complete silence when our guns were still. The endless chatter of the bugs and the occasional cry of a bird willing to live in a war zone had ended. There was no way we would bathe in the river again, which was also orange. Bright, like Orange Crush.

> "... we're all spirits, and
> Are melted into air, into thin air:
> And like the baseless fabric of this vision,
> The cloud-capp'd towers, the gorgeous palaces,
> The solemn temples, the great globe itself,
> Yea, all which it inherit, shall dissolve,
> And, like this insubstantial pageant faded
> Leave not a rack behind. We are the stuff
> As dreams are made on; ..."
>
> William Shakespeare, *The Tempest*

MEDEVACKED

Photo by Tim Page

One morning before my twelve-hour shift was to begin, a pain in my gut sped me to the deck above the pond in time to expel the previous night's dinner. But the expulsion of my fluids had just begun. I booked it to the six-seater down the hill to shit this brown stinky water, but before making it back, I threw up a pile of green bile on the side of the path. Garfield was awakened to take my place. I managed to make it down the hill a few more times until there was nothing left to leave in the crapper.

On the way up the hill from the john, our water trailer on the side of the path would beckon me like a siren. Whatever was going on, or wrong, sucked the liquid out of me. I was dehydrated and unbelievably thirsty. Because of the lack of bathrooms in this country, our water was a green-brown color and smelled like chlorine. Kool Aid was one of the most sought-after things from "the world" to mask the odorous water. My thirst was so overwhelming I would hold the spigot open and guzzle the stuff. Water was my enemy and before reaching the mini-bunker, it would violently come out in the form of this rank green bile. They wouldn't let me near FDC and Jimmy vacated his cot and moved back to the tent. This routine of drink, puke, drink, puke, continued for the rest of the day. A coke would stay down with no satisfaction, but I craved water. All I could do was lay on my cot and wait for the next episode. My friends, including Lieutenant Briggs, asked McCreedy to let me go to the Airborne Medics just up the hill, but he refused. McCreedy really didn't like me, remember? Enough men had gone home or transferred out of Charlie Battery to dismiss Lieutenant McCreedy's armed guard, but the new boys already knew he was an asshole.

By the third day, Hobbs and Garfield had seen enough and snuck me up the hill to the aid station. The two Medics jumped into action when my temperature was 104. After sticking a saline drip in my arm, they bullshitted with my friends and waited. Yikes! It was now 105 and another liter was hooked up. I could hear the two docs behind me at a loss for a cure. One came over to take my pulse. I don't know what it was, but when he let go of my hand it dropped like a rock and hung over the side of the cot. I couldn't talk or move a muscle, but I was totally aware. Finally, they called in a medevac. My friends helped some of the Airborne guys carry me down to the LZ while someone else held the liter of saline dripping in my arm.

The chopper coming to get me was shot down, so a second was dispatched to get the men from the crashed Huey before picking me up. They strapped me in next to one of the wounded men from the downed medevac and said goodbye. The man next to me was in bad shape, unable to hold my saline drip. One of the medics pulled it out before the Huey lifted off. As we banked away, Charlie Battery waved goodbye. Hold on, not so fast.

In the end, it was goodbye to most of them. After landing in Vietnam, a deal was put on the table for us. If you got home with less than three months to go, you were out. I mean OUT! Extending your time in-country to fit this timeframe was part of the offer and I jumped on it. Not too many did. Most of Charlie Battery would be home soon, including my whole section. It seemed like a long time, but I only spent a year and nine months in the U.S. Army.

A WEEK IN THE REAR

By the time we landed in Hue, I was seeing through a fog as well as thinking through one. I did remember flying over a huge swath of dead rainforest in slow motion. When I came to in the morning, a lot of wounded soldiers surrounded me in a huge canvas-covered Quonset Hut where I spent the next four days. Most of the men there were in serious condition. I watched one leave on a stretcher, his head covered with a blanket. I felt a little guilty being there for intestinal distress.

They treated me well. The fever started going down and in a day, I could hold water and on the next, a little food. I had lost twenty pounds and was still weak. After being discharged on day four and given directions to our rear area, I was able to hitchhike most of the way there.

After stumbling into our OR, I was so emaciated that Sergeant Desmond wouldn't let me go back to Bastogne, in spite of McCreedy's insistence that I return. Everything I owned was still up there—my helmet, rifle, clothes, guitar and Shakespeare. The complete works.

They set up a cot for me in headquarters next to Kibisky. Captain Gerber and First Sergeant Desmond had their own rooms in the back and the Motor Pool guys were next door. The timing was perfect to spend a few days of relative peace and quiet away from the 175s. This was an Army area next to the large Marine contingent there with good food and (heaven forbid!) showers. Kibisky loaned me a uniform so the crusty one I arrived in could be cleaned.

He also informed me about the assassination of Robert Kennedy. The tragic news of Martin Luther King's murder reached me earlier in one of the few letters I received at Bastogne. Our isolated world at the remote base became more apparent when Kibisky wished me a happy birthday which had passed me by a week earlier. I lay on my bunk for a few days and caught up on events back home in "Stars and Stripes," our primary source of news. This peaceful time in the rear area was in stark contrast to the civil unrest raging in the States. The men who could lead us out this mess were being killed and our cities were on fire. We had our own issues to deal with in Vietnam. I wouldn't truly feel the tension blistering in the U.S. until my flight home in the midst of a plane full of civilians a couple of months later.

Kibisky was an E-5 already. No wonder, he was an amazing man. He looked like Woody Allen and when he spoke, the illusion was complete. You could ask him anything about anything and most of the time he knew the answers. Which is why First Sergeant Desmond chose him to be his clerk. For that matter, Desmond was also remarkable. Most of the time, but not always, those who climbed to the top of their rank were intelligent or were great leaders. Sometimes both. They commanded your respect and usually earned it.

I read three books while gaining a little weight, became better friends with Kibisky, and got to know the First Sergeant and Captain Gerber. I needed to gain ten more pounds and after two weeks was feeling pretty good. Just in time to help pack the equipment for a road trip back to Dong Ha. Our trucks from Motor Pool convoyed to the Airborne base the day before to load the Battery's ammo, supplies, and to carry our men out of the dead land. They would leave Bastogne after daybreak and we would precede them and be set up for business by the time they arrived at Dong Ha.

I didn't have anything to pack and hoped my stuff was on the convoy and not sitting in that mini-bunker.

I was issued or loaned a flak jacket, helmet, M-16, and ammo for the trip. Garfield had retrieved my wallet with all the vehicle license and ID in time to throw it on the chopper as I lifted off from Bastogne.

I drove one of the three-quarter-tons with two replacements from Fort Sill. The other truck was also full of new men. Kibisky drove the jeep with the captain, the first sergeant, and a new lieutenant replacing McCreedy who was heading back to the states. Hopefully, for a discharge and not a promotion. A deuce-and-a-half to carry the desks and equipment rounded out our convoy.

BACK TO DONG HA

Driving the three-quarter-ton near the rear of our small procession made the return trip north considerably different from the big land march the battery made months ago. I could see everything from the high top of the APC, but now had to really concentrate to keep up with the jeep ahead that was booking it back to our original base. The truck behind me didn't seem to have any trouble keeping up, however, as it hugged my ass.

This was a big transition period for us. Our year was about up and most of the original members of Charlie Battery would be back home soon. Men were transferred to other units to allow replacements to learn their jobs. There were always new recruits to get to know and I was delivering two of them. For some reason FDC had remained intact. Specialist Five Howden left us at Dong Ha and his replacement was finally arriving with me.

We crossed the Perfume River and I got my last look at the bullet-riddled city. The boat people had moved on as we sped to Dong Ha. Our old camp had been transformed by the Navy Seabees. The hot leaky tents were replaced by wooden barracks with metal roofs and walls that went halfway up with screens covering the rest. Although incredibly loud when it rained, the leaky tents would not be missed.

I helped unload the equipment to transfer command of our unit to Dong Ha. Once the HQ was in order the replacements had to report in. After returning the borrowed battle gear, I drove the truck to Motor Pool and walked over to the new barracks where my original tent was. I picked the same northwest corner with a view of the mountains and turned the cot upside down to claim it. Hopefully, my stuff was en route from the remote airborne base by the A Shau Valley.

I don't know who surrounded our billets with sandbags, but I'll be eternally grateful. It was hard to imagine spending that much time in Bastogne. As it turned out, it was a Hell Hole.

Before the battery arrived, a truckload of replacements showed up, all of them trainees from Fort Sill, including an entire FDC section. As the new men were reporting in, the lead jeep of the convoy from Bastogne rounded the corner followed by a parade of trucks, track vehicles, and dust.

As they were fanning out to their places, I walked down to our new bunker to greet my section as they pulled up. The rear door of our APC lowered while all the diesel engines in the convoy idled. Kellerman and Murphy couldn't get out fast enough, eager to stretch their legs. Kornowski, Hobbs, and Garfield handed down their gear and climbed to the familiar dirt of Dong Ha. It felt good to see them. We had spent more than a year in tight quarters together. Even though none of us shared the same interests, we did share the work, the experience of Vietnam, and the stories of our lives. I knew these men better than most of the people I would ever know.

As Sofian was servicing the generator and we started transferring the equipment to the bunker, Lieutenant Briggs came down with the new boys. I saluted, "Good afternoon, sir." Born and raised in Detroit, Briggs was not a career soldier. His uniform as well as his hat, which had grease spots on it, wasn't as spiffy as most of the other officers. He said I had lost too much weight and was glad to see me. Apparently, my future had been questionable. He immediately ordered the new recruits to continue moving the equipment and the old crew would tell them where to put it. We watched the new boys as they worked with great enthusiasm, like most do on the first day on the job. We were aware of how much they had to learn in the upcoming week. But then again, all of us were at work, days after landing on the bay of Da Nang a year ago.

The year would be up for everyone in my section, but the officers and me. The new men were all trained in Fire Direction and Howden's replacement who rode along with me from Hue was an E-5 with experience. This was his second tour.

Sofian cut the diesel motor just in time to start the generator, which ran most of the time charging the batteries for our lights and radios. These firebases were hardly ever quiet. Motor Pool unloaded our personal belongings by the barracks while the new crew got accustomed to their work place. After the bunker was squared away, we helped the new guys carry their gear up to our quarters. We exchanged the usual information about ourselves and saw in them what we must have looked like a year ago. So far, I was still the only Californian in our battery. What were the odds? I spotted my guitar case on top of our equipment by the barracks. All of my things were lashed together, including my M-16. Even Shakespeare made the trip.

By the time we were back online, the gong from the mess tent clanged away. The cooks busted butt to put together a good meal for us. The guns were in position and all of Charlie Battery was having dinner at the same time, which was a rare occasion.

We spent the next few days familiarizing the new boys with our work procedure. Kellerman was the first to say goodbye before leaving for Cam Ranh Bay. I was on duty when Murphy, Sofian, and Kornowski came down to see us before they left for "the world." Hobbs and Garfield were informed by Kibisky the following day of their time to return home.

The last two to leave were my best friends in Vietnam. Another goodbye that seemed permanent, although Garfield would visit me over a year later. I was the doorman at a rock & roll club in Marin County called the *Lion's Share* when he tapped me on the shoulder. He was the only man from Vietnam I ever saw again.

I was one of the few left in the battery that climbed down to the landing craft in Da Nang. Desmond added another year. There were those who liked it over there. Kibisky and the First Sergeant were joined at the hip, so I wasn't surprised that he was staying to take care of him. I only knew a handful of men now. A few in the gun crews. Westmoreland extended as well as Specialist Five Nelson who added two weeks getting out early to become a veterinarian. Private Jenkins and I became friends after our trip to the dentist. He still talked about our aborted ride to Dong Ha. I guess when you've been in-country for a few days and that happens, you talk about it until you're issued a new truck without all the bullet holes.

FOOTLOOSE & FANCY-FREE

Once the original Fire Direction section went home, I reported to work in our bunker. Since our return to Dong Ha, the missions had been sporadic, mostly from motion detectors in the DMZ. This was a calm period for us. It was almost like the VC and NVA were recovering from their losses after Tet, planning their next assault. Meanwhile, the Marines had abandoned Khe Sanh and were leveling the firebase. The bare land left behind was another symbol of the futility of the Vietnam War.

I greeted the new boys and wondered what job waited for me. Lieutenant Briggs got up from his desk and motioned for me to follow him outside. As we sat on some sandbags, I wondered what was up. Maybe my Marine flak jacket sent the wrong message to the new guys. He offered me a Camel and we smoked for a bit. He looked my way and told me to get lost.

"You're done."

I didn't understand.

"I don't care what you do, but you're done with FDC. The new boys are doing fine. They're much smarter than you guys were." He grinned. "I'm serious, just pretend your tour is up. It should be easier for the new boys from here on."

I flicked the ash from my cigarette into the helmet at my feet by accident. After blowing it off, I smiled at Lieutenant Briggs. "Okay, but what will I do?"

He laughed. "You've got to be shitting me. Don't you know your nickname?"

"Flower Man?"

Briggs stood and laughed again. "You have a new one. Where's White?"

I field stripped my Camel and saluted the lieutenant. "Yes, sir! Thank you, sir."

As I walked up to the barracks, I did wonder what I was going to do and if the new guys were really that much smarter than us.

As it turned out, these were the men who would soon move to Con Tien with Charlie Battery. I can only assume that Brigg's prediction of "easier" was way off the mark.

I LOVE A PARADE

That very afternoon, as I lay on my cot staring at the mountains in the "Land of the Million Elephants and the White Parasols" unsure what my next move would be, Kibisky told me exactly what I was going to do.

"First Sergeant wants to see you, Flower Man. You're going to a parade in Da Nang." He didn't know about the arrangement Briggs had made with me. That was between us.

Desmond told me to report to the OR after breakfast in my cleanest uniform with a soft cover and no weapon. I would accompany Captain Gerber to Da Nang to represent the battalion in a big Fourth of July parade and carry the guide-on.

Kibisky told me that I was supposed to be our turret repairman after all, but Nelson wandered in before me and got the job. As it turned out, it was a stroke of luck for me, but Desmond felt bad about it. His desk was full of paperwork with all the new men building the unit back in Oklahoma, or he would have caught the mistake, I'm guessing. Maybe that's why he was always nice to me. Something you don't often call your First Sergeant. That may also be the reason he chose me to carry the guide-on. It's in the lead of a formation with an officer or NCO to the side or in front shouting cadence. If you can't hear the rhythmic commands of the cadence, which is seldom the case, the guide-on will tell you when to halt, go, double time, turn, whatever, by the way it's lifted and tilted to the sides or front.

It had been a year since I carried our colors in that big parade in Oklahoma. Lieutenant Carpenter spent hours with me until I had the art of the guide-on down, but I was really rusty.

Next day, I skipped the daily formation before breakfast and ate early by myself. The new mess sergeant introduced himself, sat down with a cup of coffee, and told me about Des Moines, Iowa. I watched the men standing at ease in the early morning darkness while the captain informed them of the day's business. This pre-dawn ritual would gladly be excluded from my daily routine, whatever that was.

After finding out more about Des Moines than anyone should know, I walked over to headquarters. Desmond was a busy man to skip chow, but I was glad he had. He was at his desk when I asked if he could give me another lesson with the guide-on. With all the replacements coming in, his head was buried in paperwork, so I think he was glad to take a break. He leaned back and propped his boots on the desk sending someone's orders to the floor. With his hands behind his head as he barked out the cadence, I marched in place while he refreshed me. Kibisky came in from breakfast and marched along with me as I pretended a broom was our flag. By the time Captain Gerber arrived, I was up to speed, I hoped.

The clerk drove us to the airfield and after another fun takeoff, I was bound for Da Nang. Captain Gerber told me I would be returning without him. After the parade, he would leave to take command of another 175 battery in the south. I wondered why Kibisky had thrown two duffle bags on the plane along with the Captain's battle gear. I was already starting to miss him. He had been one of the bright spots in our leadership.

We landed at the airport on the huge Marine base, the headquarters of I-Corps. Major Kendt, the battalion executive officer, number two in charge, and his driver were waiting with the battalion's guide-on. We sped to this big field full of thousands of Army and Marines. The Major led us to the front of one of the many formations. I looked behind me and didn't recognize anyone, plus I had no idea what was going on. Were they just a bunch of guys rounded up to represent us? Were these the B Battery boys, or what? Nerves started swelling in me with the realization the men marching behind me could be going in any direction. Our wise captain sensed my apprehension and told me to follow the lead of the flags ahead and he would help in the turns. The band set the beat, and after covering every square inch of the field, each unit marched off one by one and the parade was over. We saluted Major Kendt who then drove off in a hurry. Another jeep arrived with Captain Gerber's gear in the rear. We shook hands, saluted, and he left for his new assignment.

After standing there for a while reflecting on the whirlwind of the day's events, I was directed to a Marine mess hall for chow and a place to spend the night. I was feeling pretty impressed with myself for pulling off that marching around the field thing without a mishap until a Marine Major stepped in front of me. I stood at attention and saluted. Without returning it, he chewed me up and down about my boots. They hadn't been polished since they were issued a year ago and any trace of black was long gone. The white leather really stood out marching in the parade with all the darker ones. The Major saw them from the grandstand and couldn't wait to lay into me.

"You're carrying the colors for your company, son. Show some pride in your unit and polish those boots!"

"It's a disgrace, sir. Of course, I'll take care of it, sir. Right away, sir."

I then enjoyed a nice rear area dinner and lay on my cot to catch up on some sleep, knowing full well I would never polish my boots.

My ride to the airport found me after breakfast. Colonel Barnes was on his way home, and Major Kendt was being promoted and had assumed command of the battalion. The new CO was staying in Da Nang to catch up on Bravo Battery. His driver, however, was going north with me. His name was Dan Woods, "Just call me Woody," a motorcycle racer from San Jose and another California boy.

On the C-130 flight to Dong Ha, I told him about Lieutenant Briggs's cutting me loose. He couldn't believe it. Woody drove me right to my barracks.

"Come visit next door at Headquarters before the Colonel returns." Dan turned the jeep around and headed to Headquarters Battery.

It felt good to be back in familiar surroundings. After a hearty supper, I slept like a rock.

True to my decision about the early reveille formation, I slept in and had a late breakfast. I checked into the fire direction bunker to make sure Lieutenant Briggs had'nt been transferred and walked down to the gun pits to see some of the men I knew.

Sergeant Horner was "Back in the World" along with most of his gun crew. Willy Darnby had just received news from Kibisky about his return home and was beyond excited. He would get a two-week leave, finally marry the mother of his children, and then be stationed God knows where for the rest of his tour. I strolled over to Motor Pool and hung out with Jenkins while he changed the oil in his truck. I didn't know much about Jenkins. Every time I asked about his personal life, he would tell a joke.

"Where you from, anyway?"

"Kansas. Did you hear the one about the chicken crossing the road?"

I would have chickens on my ranch in the years to come and often thought about Private Jenkins when one ran in front of me. It was time for lunch and more news about Des Moines before an afternoon guitar session.

I was sharing the barracks with the replacements for my section. The sandbag details were completed by my heroes, so the off-duty crew didn't have much to do. I'm assuming Briggs said something to them because they never questioned what the hell I was doing there.

The next day, I set out looking for my new friend in Headquarters. Woody was easy to find and with the Colonel away was almost as footloose as me. We had lunch in their mess where he set it up for me to share guard duty with him that night.

Back in my tent, I read more of *Romeo and Juliet* and played the guitar while waiting for dinner. I was leaving the mess tent after chow on my way to Headquarters Battery, when I passed who I presumed was our new CO. I saluted, walking by with a purpose. I heard him stop but kept on walking. I pictured our new captain scratching his head and wondering, "Who is that guy?"

Woods introduced me to the sergeant of the guard and we took our places behind an M-60 pointed towards those familiar mountains. We spent the night watching the ground in front of us through the orange light cast from the illumination rounds held aloft by their parachutes. The time was filled with non-stop chatter about our past and hopeful future. We both agreed on one thing we craved besides a woman, a tall cold glass of milk and some Oreos.

He told me about his wild first week in-country. He had just been assigned to be Major Kendt's driver when one of A Battery's 175s hit a mine leaving the Rock Pile. His first job for the major was to race to the scene from Dong Ha while Kendt secured a platoon of Marines and a tank retriever on the radio. As the gun was being pulled out of the ravine it had been blown into, a spotter plane sighted a large force of NVA approaching them to capture or destroy it. Major Kendt called in six heavily armed Hueys from the First Cavalry, and after a wild firefight, they were able to get the gun to Dong Ha.

Another incident I never heard about was an artillery attack that destroyed Service Battery's facilities. Volunteers managed to save some equipment and parts, but there were numerous casualties. Not only were we blind to world events, but to what was happening in our own battalion.

It was nice having a good friend again. My buddies in the battery that were still there all had jobs to do. For all I knew I might have been the only soldier in Vietnam without one.

I was improving on the guitar and was nearing the end of the "Complete Works" when the Colonel returned. Woody was now on-call 24/7.

Soldier By Chance

I decided to get out of Dodge and visit a classmate from Aberdeen. Tom Manual was the clerk for Alpha Battery at Camp Carroll. He had extended his time in-country like me in order to leave the Army early. His life as a turret repairman was as short as mine. The clerk has one of the most important tasks and usually the smartest guy gets the job. Your desk is between the CO's and the first sergeant's, and all of the business goes through you. Kibisky was a perfect example. He knew all our addresses and phone numbers as well as each long service number by heart. You could ask about any baseball player and get their batting average. He was from Brooklyn and knew everything about the Yankees.

Tom with his Martin guitar

THE CAM LO GRAND PRIX

Next day at lunch, after a detailed description of where to boogey in Des Moines, I walked out the gate to the road and stuck my thumb out. The first truck to pass stopped and I climbed in back with a load of Marines who had been supporting Con Tien on their way back to Hue. They had been in the early fighting there with some wild stories.

They were curious why I was hitchhiking, let alone by myself. I told them about extending and Lieutenant Briggs' order to get lost. They couldn't comprehend such a thing—that I was in the Army up there also surprised them. I mentioned the trip to Con Tien for their dead comrades and how aware I was of the constant attacks the base had been under. These were the soldiers who fought door to door in Hue after Tet. They had heard of Bastogne but not of the deforestation by Agent Orange. This group of Marines had lost men all over I-Corps. They told me half the guys in the truck were replacements.

I didn't tell my best war story about storming that machine gun nest with my plastic Tommy Gun years ago.

The junction at Highway 9 came quickly and as I was climbing down from the truck, one of the soldiers asked if I was going to hitchhike home. We all laughed and they drove off.

I crossed the road and waited for someone going west. I was feeling a little pumped up after gaining the respect from a bunch of battle-hardened Marines. More amazement than respect. They were probably making odds on how long I'd last out here. After waiting a little too long, I unslung my rifle and backed out of the open into some bushes. The minutes ticked on and my recollection of this busy stretch of road was of a time gone by. If I thought I'd be on the side of the road by myself for an hour, I would definitely be on my cot reading *Hamlet*.

I hate to admit it, but the reaction the truckload of soldiers from Con Tien gave me was an ego boost. After sixty long minutes alone on the roadside, I could only picture that ego disappearing in a hail of gunfire or the crack of a single shot.

Not to worry, some trucks were coming and the first one stopped. I climbed into the empty seat by the driver, who stared at me for a while before asking where I was headed. He was also going to Camp Carroll, the difference being the driver was on his way to a company that was actually there. He told me Alpha Battery moved out a week ago as we drove through the gates of the base. It was getting late to return to Dong Ha. My road trip to visit Tom Manual was getting off to a rocky start.

He did have some good news, however. There was an empty cot in his bunker and two out of three reels of the movie *Grand Prix* with James Garner and Eva Marie Saint, would be showing that night after dinner. The cooks were good there and the movie was great even though the first reel was missing. Another lucky stroke was not staying in that rat-infested bunker I had previously visited.

I pretended there was a purpose in my presence and didn't stir up too much attention. I put the word out that I was looking for a ride to Dong Ha, not wanting to wait around the junction again. At breakfast, I was tapped on the shoulder by someone who was delivering some guys to the airbase for a flight to their R&R. Perfect. The three-quarter-ton full of happy Marines on their way to Vacation Land let me off at our gate. I wondered if my absence had been noticed. *Nobody* knew I was gone.

I spent that afternoon gazing at the hills in the distance. These mountains had fascinated me from the first days in this country. My imagination took me over them through Laos, Thailand, Burma, Bhutan, India, and to the top of the world in Nepal and China.

At dinner, the place starting buzzing because the truck that brought me in also dropped off a movie. The last two reels of *Grand Prix* with Eva Marie Saint.

FINAL DAYS

Good Morning Vietnam!

I continued my regimen of sleeping in and taking a long, late breakfast. I got to know the cooks who thought I was on some special detail. Even though the Martin was sounding better, my playing didn't allow them to think music had anything to do with it. By that time, the mess sergeant was giving me the rundown on friends and relatives in Iowa.

Soldier By Chance

One morning, I was awakened by someone kicking my cot. Tom Manual, the clerk I was going to see in Cam Lo, was standing there with the early morning sun lighting up his red hair and freckled face. We ate breakfast with the rest of the battery, but stayed long after they went to work and drank coffee sharing our stories of the past year. Manual told me about the Bronze Star he had been awarded. He killed three VC on a convoy when it was attacked, but wouldn't talk about it. We had the same apprehensions about this war back in the beer hall at Fort Sill. Those doubts had turned to conclusions for both of us.

The loss of human life and the destruction of the rainforest at Bastogne was a turning point for me. The pride Manual didn't feel for his medal made it clear to him he didn't belong here. We dropped more ordnance on Vietnam than all of our previous wars combined. When that wasn't enough, poisoning the countryside came into play. Too many on all sides were dying in a war we weren't going to win. At what price victory, when none was in sight?

I think the cooks thought I was being briefed for my special detail by this E-5 as we spent most of the morning under the mess tent drinking coffee. Manual stayed the day with us and the new boys and I wanted to know about his year in-country. We walked down the hill to see Woody. Colonel Kendt was on his way back to the US while Woody waited for the new Battalion Commander. He was on guard duty again, but would be able to drive Manual to the airport in the morning. All three of us went. Tom Manual was on his way home.

Depending on the new Colonel's whereabouts, Woody and I continued guard duty and that's where I met Mike Henderson. They were scheduled to man one of the machine guns and I just joined the nest. He was in communication at headquarters and the timing of our meeting couldn't have been better. Dan had mentioned Mike, who did yoga every night before dinner, and meditated afterwards. There was this air of confidence or something about this man from Salt Lake City that drew you to him.

Woody had become a real friend and shared the same questions I had about life, death, God, and war. We spent many a night talking about this while on guard duty. Henderson shared his answers to these uncertainties that he had gained through years of study. Mike was drawn to the Eastern religions, focusing on personal enlightenment and peaceful ways to co-exist. But in the end, he believed that war was sometimes necessary and therefore it was essential to kill. We would walk around the perimeter reading the *Bhagavad Gita*, "The Song of God," the Hindu bible. I could agree with some of that, but how did he feel about this war?

"That remains to be seen," was his reluctant answer.

I had seen enough. This philosophy clashed with the pacifist I was becoming, but it brought about a balance that would surface years later. It's unfortunate that man has rarely gotten along with his inner contradictions. Protecting cultures from outside influences creates division and conflicting beliefs spawn war. I was a foolish young man full of idealism while in Vietnam. Fifty years later, my confidence in our compatibility has been severely shaken and the divisions seem to be broadening, even in our own country. The war in Southeast Asia wouldn't erode this optimism. The shaping of a more complex world, distancing each other from unity, gradually took that idealism from me.

C-Battery's replacements were starting to stare at me when I passed. I somehow managed to stay off the new captain's radar. Instead of "Where's White?" I had become "Who's White?"

The *Complete Works of Shakespeare* were completed and I could almost play the guitar. One afternoon Kibisky sat down on my cot next to me, while I strummed my Martin. I knew why he was there even before I looked into his eyes.

"When?"

"Tomorrow morning after chow, go pick up your orders from Desmond." When I got to the OR, the first sergeant smiled and told me to come back in the morning. This was a shock. Maybe I should have kept one of those short-timer's calendars. I said goodbye to everyone I knew, not so many now. I walked over to Motor Pool to say goodbye to Westmoreland and Jenkins. The general and I wished each other luck. I can't tell you how many times this guy wanted to kick my ass at Fort Sill. I'll tell you again anyway. He was a big man from Arkansas and could have easily done it.

Jenkins was servicing his truck and was already counting the days for his return home. I told him to keep his head down, then walked down to the FDC bunker.

Lieutenant Briggs was at his desk when I sat down next to him. He ushered me outside where we sat on the same sandbags that had cooled our butts almost two months earlier. He smoked one of my Camels this time. We didn't say much again. I thanked him for being the coolest officer I would ever know. He wished me luck.

"So far, my luck has held, sir. I'm passing it on to you. If you want it."

"I'll take it, Flower Man."

The cooks were hard at work when I dropped in before dinner. I told the new mess sergeant if I was ever in Des Moines, I would look him up and I had to wait while he found a pencil to write down his address. As I walked away, I chuckled to myself realizing that a year from now most of Charlie Battery would know all about Des Moines, Iowa.

Then I booked it down to Headquarters Battery to catch Woody. The new battalion commander would arrive in a few days, leaving Mr. Woods on guard duty at night, but free in the day.

"I'll pick you up after breakfast."

I packed and reported to the OR early next day. The First Sergeant was by himself and after handing me my orders, I saluted. You're not supposed to salute an NCO but he returned it. Desmond was the heart and soul of Charlie Battery.

"Find Kibisky for a ride to the airport. Good luck in 'The World'."

"Thank you, Sergeant."

Kibisky had been one of my favorite people during that year. I told him about the ride with Woody and thanked him for his friendship. There wasn't much to take home, just my guitar and some personal things. Everything else—flak jacket, helmet, M-16, and Shakespeare lay on my cot. We drove out the gate in nonstop conversation that subsided to complete silence.

BACK IN "THE WORLD"

I did tear up a little when the C-130 made its ascent and banked away from the DMZ. I could only visualize the Colonel's jeep driving back to the base. This sadness caught me off-guard. Working, eating, playing, and bunking with eight men in tight quarters for over a year creates a bond that's unexplainable. For us, a little love, a little hate, but the bottom line was we liked and respected each other. The nostalgia would soon be replaced with the joy of stepping foot on my homeland.

I was processed-out at Cam Ranh Bay and issued a new dress uniform with all the right insignias, spec-four, I-Corps, and three ribbons—for what, I didn't know.

The next day, a commercial airliner was returning to the U.S. with a planeload of happy campers. There were stewardesses again and going home was becoming a reality.

On the long flight to McCord Air Force Base in Washington state, I sat next to an Army Ranger. He wore the black beret of the Special Forces and bloused his dress uniform above very shiny boots. He told me about blackening his face and crawling under the wire with a K-bar and slitting as many gook throats as he could. According to him, there were many. I didn't mention Flower Man and borrowed his Zippo lighter with a skull and "Dr. Death" engraved on it to light my Camel straights. This was back in the day when you could smoke and carry a gun on board an airplane.

It took all day to process out of the Army with a complete physical, lots of paperwork, name tag for my new uniform, a ride to Sea Tac Airport, and on to San Francisco.

Being the only one in uniform, sitting in the middle of a planeload of civilians gave me an uneasy feeling, especially since some were staring at me. When one of the stewardesses recognized me, it helped me settle down. Her name was Susie and she was an old girlfriend from high school. I was aware of the discontent brewing at home, but was unprepared for the cold reception everyone but Susie gave me. No one thanked me for my service. That's supposed to be a joke. I wouldn't hear that term until years later when our soldiers were dying in Iraq and Afghanistan. I think the general attitude at this time was, "You should be ashamed of your service."

During the winter of 1964, Susie had worn my namesake's black wool sweater with a red

Soldier By Chance

"N" on the front for North Eastern. Her boyfriend was waiting when we walked in from the plane. I now had a ride home. I was relieved to walk out of the airport with them. The looks coming my way weren't sympathetic. I had intended to surprise my family, so this lucky encounter gave me a ride to my old home's doorstep.

My youngest sister, Cynthia, was doing the dishes when she saw me come in the back door. It was all happening too fast. One of the plates crashed to the floor before I could greet her. I set my bag and guitar down and walked through the house to see my folks. Dad was reading a paperback and listening to loud classical music. He always did that on Sunday afternoons. He rose and just stood there, when my mother came out of the dark hallway and wrapped her arms around me.

She looked horrible. I held her thin body while she wept. For some reason, my dad was waiting for me to come home before divorcing my mom. Her much younger friend from church had been carrying on with him the past year and everyone knew it. Cynthia called my grandparents who lived close by. It wouldn't be long before they arrived.

My old room looked much the same as it did four years ago. I took off the brand-new uniform and exchanged it for some wrinkled civvies from the raggedy duffle bag that had accompanied me overseas.

This was all happening too fast. Just days ago, I was in Dong Ha, and now the U.S. Army was history. I thought about the time before college and the military that was spent in this room. My grandparents showed up while I was studying the bulletin board covered with Top Forty lists. *This was all happening too fast.*

They hoped to see me in uniform and I could see their disappointment when I refused to put it back on. My mom went back to her room while I encapsulated the past year. After Cynthia went to bed, my dad and I talked for hours about his thoughts on the war and mine. He also tried to explain his new relationship, but I didn't want to hear any of that.

I spent the next day with my mother. She understood when I told her I was hitch-hiking to the California Shakespeare Festival in Los Gatos to see friends. I hardly recognized them. Kent and Laurie who took me to see Jimi Hendrix the year before hadn't cut their since. Kent played the sitar while the cast shed their clothes and frolicked in the pool.

David Stiers let me stay with him while I reclaimed my bearings. He lived on Vallejo Street just above the topless bars along Columbus Avenue in San Francisco. A theater company called "The Committee" was also there, where David worked as an actor before becoming "Winchester" on the TV series, "MASH." You couldn't find a more vibrant area in San Francisco, but I was lonely and lost, reminding me of those first days in Basic Training.

I ended up going back to the College of Marin for another semester and one more play. I had missed the "Summer of Love" and tried to make up for it by hitchhiking to Altamont. All two-hundred-thousand of us wanted it be Woodstock, but it was far from it. Witnessing the violence of that chaotic event from the front row made it clear those days were over. I borrowed a hundred dollars using my Martin guitar as collateral and hitchhiked to Southern Mexico for two months. A hundred dollars went a long way in those days.

When I returned to California from Mexico, a check was waiting for me. I had requested the Army to withhold one half of my paycheck each month. By the time I was discharged, it was a tidy sum. I acquired the necessary tools and worked as a carpenter.

I moved to the woods, practiced yoga, and became a successful carpenter. I acted in or directed over forty plays, six of them by Shakespeare. I carved out a ranch on two hundred acres in the foothills of the Sierra with a few horses, donkeys, and a lot of goats. I had vowed to never have a gun. After one of my baby goats was hauled off by a mountain lion, I bought a 30-30 Winchester to protect them. When a few scary incidents happened late at night, a Colt 45 Auto was added to my arsenal with the sole purpose of defending my family from men. To let those without regard for life or morality run roughshod was not an option.

Thinking back on those suicide sappers who died in our minefield at C-1, I didn't know then why they would sacrifice their lives, but I can understand it now. Peace and love is a great notion. Unfortunately, the human species seems incapable of sustaining such lofty ideals.

You think you've figured things out and sometimes you refigure them. I didn't talk about Vietnam for a good twenty years. My experiences were tame compared to most. I harbored a sense of guilt by simply having been there. As time passed, I realized how much Vietnam had shaped my being.

I regretted missing the days of the flower child before Altamont. Now, I'm glad I went to Vietnam. It might take a while, but there are lessons to be learned in war that the summer of love cannot teach.

*And as the morning steals upon the night,
Melting the darkness so their rising senses
Begin to chase the ignorant fumes that mantle
Their clearer reason.*

William Shakespeare, *The Tempest*

Distinguished Village Elders of Indochina circa 1900 - antique postcard

A BRIEF HISTORY OF INDOCHINA

There were many cultures interspersed throughout Southeast Asia with completely different customs, clothing, diets and religions. Dozens of tribes had lived there for thousands of years. The Viet kingdoms were influenced by the Chinese to the north whereas India's political and religious customs shaped the major civilizations of mainland Southeast Asia. Funan was the dominant power in the first century. They built the canals in Vietnam's Mekong Delta to control floods and limit saltwater from intruding. The southern state prospered by being on the trade route between India and China. The Khmer people of Chenla overthrew the Funan in the sixth century. The powerful Khmer Empire emerged from the Land Chenla in the middle Mekong Valley, the Water Chenla from Cambodia, and the Mekong Delta, and made Angkor its capital. They built the royal center of Angkor Wat in the ninth century on the Plain of the "Great Lake," the Tonle Sap in present day Cambodia. In the rainy season the Tonle Sap River, a tributary of the Mekong, the River of Nine Dragons, swells the Great Lake to seven times its normal area. After heavy rains, the river reverses course to do this. The surrounding farmlands are enriched by the nutrient-laden water and makes the lake one of the worlds' most productive fishing grounds.

The Dai Viet expelled the Chinese from Vietnam in the tenth century, but their influence, although not welcomed by the Vietnamese, made them some of the best farmers in Indochina.

The Hindu civilization of Champa struggled for 1,200 years to remain independent of the expanding Dai Viet and Khmer kingdoms. In 1177, the Chams sailed up the Mekong and defeated the Khmer on the "Great Lake" and sacked Angkor Wat. Champa then joined forces with the Dai Viet to fend off the invading army of Kublai Kahn. Two hundred years later, the Chams succumbed to its former ally as the Vietnamese moved south.

The Siamese ravaged Angkor in 1431, and the Khmer abandoned their capital allowing the jungle to take over.

In Cambodia, Laos, Thailand, and Burma, Buddhism is the dominant religion. There was a significant difference in the religious make-up of Vietnam. Most people there practice variations of Buddhism in conjunction with Confucianism and Taoism. There were also millions of Roman Catholics. Caodaism, a synthesis of the four previously mentioned religions, also had many followers.

Soldier By Chance

As European nations competed to colonize Asia, the French created the Union of Indochina in the mid-1800s after twenty years of armed persuasion. Except for the occupation by the Japanese during WWII, Cambodia, Laos, and Vietnam were under French control until 1953. Defeated by the Viet Minh led by Ho Chi Minh, the colonists returned to France and Algeria, leaving a vacuum that would take twenty-five years to resolve. Ho Chi Minh had attended Harvard and was first drawn to the U.S. to help support his new government. It had been less than ten years since the end of WWII when the British and the US handed Indochina back to France. In spite of Ho Chi Minh's support before the war, we rejected Vietnam's advances, and I suppose their logical reaction was to embrace the more than eager Communist nations to the North.

The Geneva Convention called for elections, which Ho would have won with a landslide. In 1956, we chose not to take the moral high ground and wouldn't sanction the elections, aligning instead with the rich and corrupt Diem Brothers who had prospered during the country's unrest. Vietnam was divided, with the northern half ruled by the Communists, while the South was governed by a military dictatorship supported by the United States. In the early 1960s, we went to South Vietnam as advisors to help stem the tide of Communism from the North. It wasn't long before it was a full blown war and our ships and planes were delivering troops and equipment on a daily basis. We were curtailed by our politics and a fear of drawing Russia and China directly into the conflict. I don't believe our objectives on how to win it were very clear. Contributing to the futility, the South Vietnamese government was so corrupt and ineffective, we had the Diem Brothers assassinated and installed Colonel Thieu as the country's leader.

With the stalemate of our involvement in the war smoldering, we resumed bombing the North and invaded Cambodia to oust the North Vietnamese along the border, but instead drove them deeper into the country where they allied themselves with Pol Pot and the Khmer Rouge. In 1970 Prince Norodom Sihanouk was deposed by the Cambodian Parliament and joined Pol Pot in opposition to the U.S. backed military regime governing his country. From 1969 to 1973, we bombed North Vietnamese sanctuaries along the border killing 150,000 Cambodian peasants.

When the opposition to the war at home reached a fever pitch, we abandoned Vietnam with our tail between our legs.

Fifty-six thousand of our soldiers had perished, along with 1.2 million Vietnamese. In 1975, after our withdrawal, Pol Pot's teenage guerrilla army marched into Cambodia's capital, Phnom Penh, and took control. He began to create an agrarian utopia inspired by Mao Zedong's Cultural Revolution in China, a disaster for both countries.

The renamed Democratic Republic of Kampuchea began to purge itself from all outside influences. Foreign embassies closed along with TV stations and newspapers. Radios and bicycles were confiscated, businesses shuttered, religions banned, and parental authority revoked. The cities, along with Phnom Penh's two million inhabitants, were evacuated at gunpoint. On the way to the countryside, 20,000 died. They were forced into slave labor, working from 4 AM to 10 PM, with two rest periods. Pol Pot's young soldiers were eager to kill anyone for the slightest infraction.

The Khmer Rouge conducted a reign of terror that rivaled any of the twentieth century. The Turks came close to eradicating the Armenians in the early 1900s. Stalin's political purges killed millions in Russia, along with Germany's attempt to rid the world of the Jews. Pol Pot's murderous campaign did not equal the dead count of the atrocities carried out by Stalin and Hitler, but it was devastating for Cambodia. Most foreigners were executed, but the dividing line of who lived or died depended on your education. Basically, if you could spell your name, your body was dumped in "The Killing Fields." The relocated population were forced to become farmers and a good portion of them starved to death.

The teenage army also continued the destruction of Angkor Wat to destroy its cultural significance. Angkor was one of the most magnificent ancient cities on earth. Its beauty and sophistication rivaled that of Egypt, Persia, Greece, Rome, and the civilizations of the Americas, such as the Aztec, Maya, and Inca.

In 1978, Vietnam invaded Cambodia to stop border attacks, defeated the Khmer Rouge, and in 1979, Phnom Penh fell. Pol Pot retreated to Thailand and began a guerrilla war against a succession of Cambodian governments. China supported Pol Pot and the Khmer Rouge. In 1979, the Chinese attacked Vietnam in response to their invasion of Cambodia and got their ass kicked in short order. Peace would not return to Southeast Asia for another ten years.

THOMAS WHITE

Thomas White was born in 1946 and grew up in Marin County, just north of San Francisco. After two years of college, he was drafted in 1966 and sent to Vietnam. Somewhat disillusioned after returning home from the war, he let go of his dream of becoming an art teacher and built houses as a carpenter.

After working in the Bay Area for six years, Tom bought two hundred acres of remote and undeveloped land in the rugged foothills of the Sierra Nevada. Over the next forty years, Lightning Ridge Ranch slowly became a real one, with a house, barns, horses, and goats. His handcrafted home on the high ridge offered commanding views of rolling hills, perennial creeks, and distant mountains. His Gold Country landscape was wrapped in lush stands of pine and oak. While working the Ranch, he also established himself as an artist, actor, and woodworker.

In 1993, the Old Gulch Fire burned for five days and reached the edge of Tom's property. In 2015, the Butte Fire roared onto the Ranch taking more than 150 acres. His herd of goats had kept the brush down and saved his house and barns. In 2016, he sold the land he loved and moved to the Gold Rush town of Murphys, California.

Tom's Lightning Ridge Ranch had been reduced to a charred wasteland, bringing back haunting memories of Vietnam.

Some memories never fade.

GLOSSARY

APC	Armored Personnel Carrier
ARVN	Army of the Republic of Vietnam
AWOL	Absent without Leave
Azimuth	Elevation/Position of the Gun Barrel
Battalion	Three Gun Batteries, Headquarters & Service Battery
Battery	Artillery Equivalent to a Company
Bouncing Betty	Mine that Pops up Before Detonating
C-Rations	Meals Ready to Eat in a Box
Cadence	A Rhythmic Flow of Sounds in Language
Chief of Smoke	The NCO in Charge of All Four Guns
Claymore	Directional Surface Mine on Perimeter
CO	Commanding Officer
Concertina	Barbed Wire on a Roll
Connex	Large Steel Shipping Containers
Cover	Hat or Helmet
Deflection	Side-to-Side Position of the Gun Barrel
DMZ	Demilitarized Zone
FDC	Fire Direction Center
FO	Forward Observer

Grunt	Infantry
Gun Bunny	Cannoneer
H&I	Harassment & Interdiction
Honcho	Boss
HQ	Headquarters
K Bar	Large Sheath Knife
LST	Landing Craft
LZ	Landing Zone
Medevac	Helicopter Ride to the Hospital
MET	Meteorological Information for Target Calculation
MOS	Job Description
MPC	Military Payment Certificate – Money
NCO	Non-Commissioned Officers – Sergeants
NVA	North Vietnamese Army Regulars
Projo	Artillery Projectile
Punji Stakes	Pointed Stakes in Hidden Pits
RPG	Rocket-Propelled Grenade Launcher
RTO	Radio Telegraph Operator
Sapper	Enemy Suicide Attacker with Explosives

www.ingramcontent.com/pod-product-compliance
Lightning Source LLC
Chambersburg PA
CBHW061142010526
44118CB00026B/2846